ACHIEVING
EYPS

Leading Practice in Early Years Settings

Second edition

Mary E. Whalley and Shirley Allen

Series editors: Lyn Trodd and Gill Goodliff

LearningMatters

First published in 2008 by Learning Matters Ltd
Reprinted in 2008, 2009 and 2010

This edition published in 2011

British Library Cataloguing in Publication Data
A CIP record for this book is available from the British Library.

ISBN: 978 0 85725 327 9

This book is also available in the following ebook formats:

Adobe ebook	ISBN: 978 0 85725 329 3
EPUB ebook	ISBN: 978 0 85725 328 6
Kindle	ISBN: 978 0 85725 330 9

Cover design by Phil Barker
Text design by Code 5 Design Associates Ltd
Project management by Swales & Willis
Typeset by Swales & Willis Ltd, Exeter, Devon
Printed and bound in Great Britain by Short Run Press Ltd, Exeter, Devon

Learning Matters Ltd
20 Cathedral Yard
Exeter EX1 1HB
Tel: 01392 215560
info@learningmatters.co.uk
www.learningmatters.co.uk

FSC
www.fsc.org
MIX
Paper from
responsible sources
FSC® C014540

Dedication

This book is dedicated to the memory of my daughter,
Anna Whalley-Moutter (1976–2005), who herself was a dedicated
professional, committed always to 'best practice' in everything she
did, including sharing teaching and learning with young children.

Contents

List of figures

List of tables

Foreword from the series editors

Each book in this series (Achieving Early Years Professional Status) focuses on under-pinning aspects of the EYP role. To support students' professional development towards achieving EYPS the contents foreground links to the current EYP Standards. This book, *Leading Practice in Early Years Settings*, is one of the series. It will be of interest to all those following courses that lead to the award of Early Years Professional Status (EYPS) and also for students on Sector-Endorsed Early Years Foundation Degree programmes and undergraduate Early Childhood Studies degree courses as these awards are key routes towards EYPS. The first edition of this book, published in 2008, proved to be very popular because it tackled leadership from the point of view of leadership of practice, exploring how leaders can change and develop their settings by changing and developing themselves and by modelling excellent practice alongside more traditional leadership approaches. In addition, the book's unusual perspective offers a valuable resource for students who are following other leadership programmes, such as the National Professional Qualification in Integrated Centre Leadership (NPQICL) and the New Leaders in Early Years programmes.

The graduate EYP role has been recognised as a key strategy in commitments of successive governments who aim to improve the quality of Early Years care and education in England. The publication of recent reports: Frank Field's Report from the independent report on a review on Poverty and Life Chances 'The Foundation Years: Preventing poor children becoming poor adults' published in December 2010; Graham Allen's independent report to Her Majesty's Government 'Early Intervention: The Next Steps' published in January 2011 and Dame Clare Tickell's independent report on the Early Years Foundation Stage to Her Majesty's Government 'The Early Years: Foundations for life, health and learning' published in March 2011; has underlined the important responsibilities that Early Years Professionals have for early interventions in the lives of vulnerable children. The reports have confirmed the need for high-quality, well-trained and educated professionals to work with the youngest children, particularly when children are disadvantaged or vulnerable in order to improve their life chances.

This book is a significant contribution to the extensive, general discourse of leadership. This edition has been updated and developed further by Mary E. Whalley and Shirley Allen. It offers important new thinking about *leadership of practice* in Early Years settings and discusses and explores this theme in diverse contexts reflecting the range of professional backgrounds of EYPs. Throughout the book authentic case studies and reflective tasks are used to deepen readers' learning. The final chapter looks at professional development beyond the achievement of Early Years Professional Status and considers how such development can refine and re-define leadership of practice.

Leading Practice in Early Years Settings greatly extends our understanding of this fundamental feature of the EYP role and we are delighted to commend it to you.

Lyn Trodd and Gill Goodliff
May 2011

About the authors and series editors

Shirley Allen
Shirley Allen is a Senior Lecturer in Early Childhood Studies at Middlesex University. In this role, she is co-leader of the Early Years Professional Status programme and is a tutor on the Early Childhood Studies Degree. She has previously worked in teacher education on undergraduate and PGCE programmes at the University of Hertfordshire. A former primary school teacher, she taught for a number of years in London schools and was a deputy head of an infant school. Her research interests are in the areas of mentoring, outdoor play and children's literacy development in the Early Years.

Gill Goodliff
Gill Goodliff is a Senior Lecturer and Head of Awards for Early Years at the Open University where she has developed and chaired courses on the Sector Endorsed Foundation Degree and as a Lead Assessor for Early Years Professional Status. Her professional work with young children and their families was predominantly in the voluntary sector. Her research interests centre on the professional identities of Early Years practitioners and young children's spirituality.

Lyn Trodd
Lyn Trodd is a Principal Lecturer and Head of Partnerships and Ventures and Undergraduate Programmes at the University of Hertfordshire. She is currently Chair of the Sector-Endorsed Foundation Degree in Early Years national network. Lyn was a member of Children's Workforce Development Council reference group consulted about the new status for Early Years Professionals and led a team which piloted EYPS at the University of Hertfordshire. Her research is focused on graduate roles for members of the Children Workforce and how professional learning programmes develop self-efficacy in participants.

Mary E. Whalley
Mary E. Whalley is a lecturer on the Foundation Degree and BA (Hons) Young Children's Learning and Development at Leeds Metropolitan University and Harrogate College. She also works as an independent consultant in Early Years practice. Drawing on many years experience as a teacher in primary schools, including special education, over the last 15 years Mary has had close involvement in the development of the Early Years workforce, including leading a DfES-sponsored research project on work-based learning. Currently, Mary combines her roles in lecturing and consultancy with that of assessor of Early Years Professional Status with Best Practice Network. Her research interests include the leadership aspect of the EYP role and children's workforce development in England.

Acknowledgements

The first edition of this book was written at a time of huge excitement and anticipation as the new graduate role of Early Years Professional was rolled out and the first EYPs were acknowledged. This second edition has been written against a backcloth of change as we waited to see what priority the new government in the UK would give to Early Years practice and provision. Nevertheless, despite the uncertainties faced, what has continued to impress me greatly is the dedication and professionalism of those working as EYPs. Coming from different parts of the country and in different work contexts, some already with EYPS and others on various pathways towards the status, I record my heartfelt thanks to all those wonderful practitioners who have been willing to share their experiences and expertise – much of which has been used in the form of case studies in this edition. At the time of writing, it is heartening to hear government endorsement that 'a highly skilled workforce is critical' for effective provision in the Early Years (Teather, 2011). So – highly skilled workforce! – this book is essentially *from* you and *for* you!

My sincere thanks, again, to Shirley Allen of Middlesex University, who has taken responsibility for Chapters 5 and 8 and has provided helpful feedback on my own writing. We have managed to meet face-to-face only occasionally but have established a good, working rapport and shared many late-night emails! Shirley has managed to support me in writing this book even while juggling the huge demands of managing the EYPS programme at Middlesex and her wider involvement in the developing children's workforce. Her support and guidance has been deeply appreciated.

My colleagues at Harrogate College, Leeds Metropolitan University and within the Best Practice Network have all been highly supportive and affirming as I've undertaken this second edition and I have valued my conversations with them and the ideas they have shared. My deep thanks must also be recorded to Lyn Trodd and Gill Goodliff, the series editors, who had the original ideas for this book and others relating to EYPS. I thank them both for the initial confidence they showed in me to begin writing in the first place and for their constant encouragement throughout this second edition. Once again, Julia Morris and Jennifer Clark have been consistently helpful and responsive through all stages of writing and I thank them sincerely, too.

Finally – as in the first edition – my profound gratitude goes to my husband, Ernie, daughters, Sara and Rachel, and grandchildren Nia and James, who have continued to give me their unstinting support, endured my distractedness and surrounded me with their love and care as I focused on the writing. I cannot thank them enough.

Mary E. Whalley
Leeds, May 2011

1 Leadership of practice: the role of the Early Years Professional

C H A P T E R   O B J E C T I V E S

This chapter provides a rationale for the book, signposts some of the topics raised in later chapters and begins to explore some of the differences between 'leadership' and 'management'. The concept of the Early Years Professional is discussed in the light of the European model of 'social pedagogue' and pedagogical leadership. Key characteristics of a leader as a supportive and interactive role model and instigator of change are outlined and some of the defining characteristics of the 'leader of practice' are suggested. Reflective tasks, case studies and self-assessment activities are included in the chapter so that you can begin to explore your role as a leader of the practice of others and gather the evidence of this role that you will need in order to achieve Early Years Professional Status.

After reading this chapter you should be able to:
- reflect on the concept of leadership in Early Years practice;
- appraise critically the role of the pedagogue and its potential as a model for the leader of practice;
- begin to apply an appropriate understanding of leadership of practice to your own role as you prepare to meet the Standards for Early Years Professionals.

This chapter is wide-ranging and will help you to reflect on how you influence and lead the practice of others in relation to most of the Standards for Early Years Professionals.

Introduction

Early Years Professional Status was a new strategic leadership role introduced by the New Labour Government in 2006 and viewed as key to improving workforce skills, knowledge and competencies and raising the quality of young children's experiences in the Early Years (Children's Workforce Development Council [CWDC], 2010a). At the time of writing, there are already over 6,000 Early Years Professionals (EYPs) working in a range of private, voluntary, independent and children's centre settings – and beyond. EYPs hold a full bachelor degree and have demonstrated that they have met all of the 39 Standards defined for the role (CWDC, 2010a). Moreover, they have provided clear evidence of these Standards both through their own practice and in their leadership and support of others and, distinctively, with babies up to the age of 18 months, toddlers up to the age of 3 years and young children from 3–5 years.

It is this 'leadership of practice' which is a defining element of the role. Many different examples of leadership of practice have continued to emerge which illustrate the diverse facets of the role. Indeed, one of the current challenges to the role is this very diversity, with EYPs to be found in widely different posts including: room leader in a private day nursery; voluntary pre-school supervisor; assistant manager of a children's centre; teaching assistant in an independent school; a family support worker; child minder; an independent consultant; and Early Years trainer.

There are a number of routes to EYPS, determined to a large extent by the qualification and experience of the individual, though not all providers offer the full range of pathways.

- Validation only – around 4 months

- Short pathway – around 6 months

- Long pathway – around 15 months

- Full pathway – around 12 months

- Early Childhood Studies Degree to EYPS Pathway – 18 to 24 months

(CWDC, 2010b)

You might well be about to embark on one of these pathways yourself and it is important that you think carefully about your emerging role as a leader of practice. Other concepts of leadership also have their place in the contemporary Early Years workforce, such as the national Professional Qualification for Integrated Centre Leadership (NPQICL) and the National Professional Qualification for (school) Headships (NPQH). While these offer valid pathways for leadership development and training (these are both qualifications while Early Years Professional is a *status*), they are models that best fit leadership of an *organisation*. In the first edition of this book, we put forward strong arguments for urgent clarification of the EYP role – especially given the juxtaposition of the developing children's centre agenda with the emergence of the EYP role. It is important that you are clear about the kind of leadership you must demonstrate and how this differs from 'management' of a setting. We continue to suggest here that the European model of social pedagogue offers insights into the EYP role. While this has been challenged by some, such as Lloyd and Hallet (2010), we believe that there is still much we can learn from that role about the essence of EYPS.

What is leadership?

Leadership is a complex subject that is often misunderstood (Horne and Stedman Jones, 2001). Almost two decades ago, Cuban (1988: 190) conducted research into leadership in schools and concluded that there are 'more than 350 definitions of leadership, but no clear and unequivocal understanding as to what distinguishes *leaders* from *non-leaders*'. If anything, the situation is even more complex today, with a diverse range of settings catering for the needs of children. However, 'leadership' is a term that is applied within many professions and most organisations and, from the outset, it is important to attempt to distinguish 'leadership' from 'management'. Confusingly, the two terms are often used interchangeably and distinctive definitions are hard to establish, especially as they are often linked in Early Years practice. Indeed some theorists (Hall, 1996) have argued that research shows it is unethical to separate leadership from management:

> *Leadership is a philosophy in action and management is an integral part. The women heads (in the study) were therefore simultaneously leaders and managers. Managing without leadership was unethical; leadership without management was irresponsible.*
>
> (Hall, 1996: 11)

The leadership element of the EYP role, however, does not inherently link together leadership with management. While acknowledging the usefulness to the role of some management *skills*, the EYP is essentially to be a leader of high-quality practice.

REFLECTIVE TASK

What do you understand by the terms 'leadership' and 'management'?

- *How different are the two concepts/roles in your experience?*

- *Think of experiences when you were well led, or well managed. How did you know that your leader/manager was doing a good job?*

- *Have there been times when you felt you were experiencing poor or inadequate leadership or management?*

- *Can you begin to identify factors that influenced your experience?*

Law and Glover (2000, cited in Rodd, 2006) offer helpful insights into the different emphases of the two roles.

Table 1.1 Managers and leaders

Managers:	Leaders:
Plan and make decisions	Give direction
Organise and clarify work	Offer inspiration
Coordinate the organisation	Build teamwork
Control and monitor the organisation's effectiveness	Set an example
	Gain respect and acceptance

(Rodd, 2006: 20)

Leadership in the Early Years

A more detailed review of the available literature on leadership in the Early Years is offered in the next chapter. However, in seeking to establish a new understanding of a leader of practice, it is important to consider here the perspectives of some of the key writers on leadership in the Early Years as you seek to clarify your own role in leading practice.

Solley (2003), from her position of nursery headteacher, suggests that the distinctive difference between leadership and management is quite clear: management involves *maintenance and oversight* of an organisation, whereas leadership is more to do with *enhancement, improvement and development.* This implies that leadership and management 'complement each other' (Smith and Langston, 1999: 6). However, it is important that you realise that the focus for the new role of EYP foregrounds *leadership.*

Leadership of practice

Moyles (2006) believes that concepts of leadership and management have yet to be fully explored in an Early Years context. Although discussing mainly leadership of an organisation, rather than of *practice,* one of the difficulties Moyles identifies is that of finding an appropriate title for the 'head' of an Early Years setting. In some, especially in the private sector, the head is usually described as a 'manager'. In the voluntary sector, she is a 'leader' or 'supervisor'. In a children's centre, there is a leader/manager – who may well have completed the National Professional Qualification for Integrated Centre Leadership (NPQICL) – and may also be an Early Years 'teacher' who has **not** completed the NPQICL but is usually viewed as the leader of practice. In many settings – particularly in the private, voluntary and independent sector – the leader and manager are the same person. Are you confused? Little wonder! In fact, you have a key role in this because, as the EYP role develops, it is EYPs themselves who are helping to shape our understanding of leadership. Cable, Goodliff and Miller (2007) suggest that you do not need to be a passive recipient in workforce reform but, rather, an active agent in developing a new sense of professional identity.

CASE STUDY

Leadership and management

Andrea, EYP: '*In the course of 15 years, I have worked as a teacher in a Reception class, a supervisor in a voluntary pre-school and as a registered childminder in my own home. I have had significant experience of working with children within the birth to five age range and last year became the coordinator for the local childminding network, organising professional development and training events for childminders. In most of the roles I have held, I believe there have been aspects of both leadership and management. In my present role, I make sure all runs smoothly in the network, just as I did as a teacher in school and as pre-school supervisor. These are "management" tasks. But I also see it important to be innovative and plan for change and this requires "leadership" skills.*'

Reflecting on the different roles she has held over the years, Andrea is able to identify the key aspects of her role where she is a leader and an initiator of change. However, not all EYPs are able to recognise opportunities for leadership quite so clearly. Use the following task to identify, within your context and setting, the opportunities you have to lead and improve practice.

Finding evidence of leadership of practice

1. Take a piece of paper and divide it into four equal parts and then further divide these sections into 2 columns.

2. Each of the four parts will represent different aspects of your role: your work with children; your work within a team of practitioners; your work in partnership with parents and carers; and your work with other professionals (see Figure 1.1).

3 In the first column of each section identify where you recognise you are already demonstrating leadership of practice and initiating change. In the second column, try to identify further opportunities to develop this.

Work with children		Work with parents and carers	
Now ?	Further opportunities	Now ?	Further opportunities
Work within staff team		Work with other professionals	
Now ?	Further opportunities	Now ?	Further opportunities

Figure 1.1 Working with others

This exercise offers you a strong reminder that EYPs do not operate in isolation. The EYP Standards themselves are grouped to demonstrate the collaborative and interactive nature of the role, for instance S25–28 relate to interaction with children, S33–36 to team-work and collaboration, and so on. ***Who*** you are 'leading' will impact on ***how*** you lead. Although set in the context of NPQICL, Margy Whalley (2005a: 7) defines this as a 'community development approach', with the setting viewed as a 'learning community' which recognises the inter-relatedness of the children, families, staff and wider community. Within the learning community, the leader has the opportunity to address the following elements:

- developing the individual's capacity to be self-directing;
- helping individuals to gain more control over their lives;
- raising self-esteem;
- promoting learning as a life-long learning experience;
- equality of opportunity;
- pushing boundaries;
- 'constructive discontent' – not having to put up with things because it's 'just the way they are';
- encouraging people to feel they have the power and confidence to change things;
- self-fulfilment.

(Whalley, 2005a)

REFLECTIVE TASK

- *Are there similarities between this list and yours?*

- *What do you make of the notion of 'constructive discontent' as a trigger for change? Are you able to identify an example from your own practice where collectively staff identified and worked together to effect change?*

Within the 'learning community', then, each member of the staff team needs be involved in contributing to change in practice. One very important aspect of the role of the leader of practice here is to model a positive disposition to change, demonstrating a clear 'hands-on' approach and showing others what is possible in the development and enhancement of practice. We might call this 'visible leadership', which is dependent on effective engagement between the leader and other staff. Think here of Albert Bandura's social learning theory (1977) which suggests that children will (unconsciously) model their own behaviour on those with whom they have a close and trusting relationship. This can be applied to your role as EYP, too. Remember that while most people within your sphere of influence will – consciously and unconsciously – take note of what you *do*, those with whom you have forged a positive relationship will also *imitate* your practice. This brings both privilege and responsibility.

REFLECTIVE TASK

Take a few moments to think about some of those significant to your own professional formation and development and who have influenced you.

REFLECTIVE TASK CONTINUED

- *In what ways do you believe they modelled effective practice and you imitated this?*

- *How might you use these reflections to enhance your own opportunities as a role model within your own leadership of practice?*

Leadership behaviours

By now you should be developing a clearer awareness of how the existing models and concepts of leadership do not quite fit what is needed for the Early Years Professional role. However, Rodd (2006) offers helpful insights in her description of leadership as a 'holistic, inclusive and empowering process'. This reminds us of the interactive behaviour of leaders of practice, where a sense of community is established, all feel valued, respected and included, and diversity is embraced.

- **Vision behaviour:** envisioning change and taking risks to bring it about.

- **Values behaviour:** building trust and openness.

- **People behaviour:** building caring relationships, with respect for individual differences.

- **Influence behaviour:** the capacity to work collaboratively.

(Adapted from Rodd, 2006: 33)

This emphasis on leadership as a range of *behaviours* further reinforces the importance of modelling high-quality practice.

REFLECTIVE TASK

Look particularly at S25, 30, 33, 34, 35, 36 and 39. Using a similar grid to that suggested on page 5, write down the opportunities you have to demonstrate these leadership behaviours in the context of each of these Standards. Reflect on further opportunities you might develop here.

Leadership qualities

Moyles (2006) has defined the Effective Leadership and Management Scheme – Early Years (ELMS–EY) using the metaphor of a tree with four distinct branches: leadership qualities; management skills; professional attributes; and personal characteristics and attitudes. The ELMS–EY model is essentially a tool by which practitioners who lead/manage Early Years settings can evaluate their own effectiveness and is particularly appropriate for those following the NPQICL route. It is

notable, however, that Moyles does differentiate here between leadership qualities and management skills; and the leadership qualities' 'branch' (complete with 'stem' and 'leaves') of the ELMS-EY nonetheless offers very helpful indicators of leadership which can be applied specifically to leadership of practice.

You may find Moyles' characteristics of effective Early Years leadership helpful as you reflect on your own role: In what ways are you:

- visionary?
- responsible for and thoughtful about basic needs: of children, staff families and setting?
- accountable for quality?
- charismatic, with integrity, engaging others, commanding and offering respect and motivating staff?
- flexible and versatile?
- knowledgeable and an informational resource for the staff?
- aware of the importance of shared values?
- able to lead and manage change?
- empower and enable all relevant people?
- a culture setter?

(Adapted from Moyles, 2006: 21–22)

Effective leadership of practice

Without doubt, the work of Siraj-Blatchford, with others, has been influential in shaping our understanding of leadership in the Early Years (Siraj-Blatchford et al., 2002; Sylva et al., 2004). Most recently, Siraj-Blatchford has collaborated with Manni (2007) on researching Effective Leadership in the Early Years sector (the ELEYS study). Their aim was to identify the characteristics or patterns of leadership that can be identified in settings judged to be offering the highest quality early learning experiences for children and families. Here is a rigorous approach to determining just what kind of leaders – and leadership skills – contribute to the best practice in Early Years provision. Although the ELEYS study adopts a much broader understanding of leadership than that appropriate for the leader of practice, there are insights here that are impacting on our under-standing of EYP leadership, especially the notion of 'building a learning community and team culture' (Siraj-Blatchford and Manni, 2007: 21). This concept of 'continuous engagement with staff in professional practice' is also one of the key elements identified as part of the NPQICL role of 'pedagogical leadership' (Whitaker, 2004: 8) The parallels between the EYP role and that of pedagogue in many European countries are explored a little later in the chapter.

Leadership of practice in a variety of settings

The model of leadership of practice required for EYPS is one that should fit across all types of Early Years settings and sit equally comfortably in a home setting, a voluntary pre-school in a small village hall, a private nursery or a large children's centre. Thus, as we have established, it is important that this distinctive model or paradigm of leadership is the 'best fit' for Early Years Professional Status. You bring to the role a wide range of professional experience and qualifications but common ground is found when each of you takes the opportunity to reflect on your own strengths and to identify appropriate and often innovative ways of demonstrating leadership by inspiring others.

The role of EYP is an aspirational one, in which the EYP seeks to demonstrate and model the highest possible commitment to quality Early Years practice and to lead and improve the practice of others across the Early Years Foundation Stage (EYFS). However, it is important to remember that you are a diverse group of people, drawn from different professional backgrounds, working in a range of different roles within maintained, private, voluntary and independent settings, and each of you will select your own way to evidence the EYP Standards from the perspective of your own particular context.

Consider some EYP candidates here:

Elizabeth *has a degree in Drama and trained as a secondary school teacher but has become increasingly fascinated by how young children learn and develop. She has decided on a career change and is on her first placement with 3–4 year olds on the full pathway EYP programme. She is using her skills in drama to encourage the pre-school team to see the potential of using story in dramatic form with young children.*

Aliya *has a background in social work but for the past three years has been employed as team member of a Children's Centre in a culturally diverse urban area. Her work includes twice-weekly toy library sessions, and leading lunchtime parent and toddler sessions and crèche provision while parents attend English or Computing Skills classes.*

Joe *is room leader in a private nursery and had the opportunity to complete a Sector Endorsed Foundation Degree in Early Years and then 'top-up' to a BA (Hons) Childhood Studies degree while he continued to work. Three colleagues work with Joe in the pre-school room which caters for up to 20 children at any one session.*

Debbie *is a graduate nurse, with previous experience of working in a private nursery setting, who is currently working as the childminder of a baby of eight months, a three-year-old boy and a four-year-old girl. Her close friend, Anna, is also a childminder in the locality and Debbie and Anna meet regularly together and bring their charges. Anna has only just started her Early Years training and often asks Debbie for advice about her practice.*

REFLECTIVE TASK

Try not to focus on the obvious differences in each of these cases. Instead, can you identify anything that these EYPs have in common in the way they are demonstrating leadership of practice?

Consider again the contexts of these EYPs and then reflect on your own. Are you able to identify further examples of evidence of your own skills in leading others' practice?

The pedagogue role

When the CWDC first produced its draft proposals for the new professional status in the developing children's workforce (CWDC, 2005) two possible titles were mooted:

- **New teacher** – signifying a specialist Early Years teacher qualification similar to that in operation in New Zealand and Spain.

- **Social pedagogue** – drawing specifically on the Danish model of Early Years graduate professionals. Across Denmark it is social pedagogues who are the main workers in nurseries and other children's settings. Other continental European countries operate a similar system, with a shared understanding of the role, though in some the role is known simply as the 'pedagogue'. Some countries also include working with teenagers and adults as part of the social pedagogue role.

For a wide range of reasons, following consultation on the draft proposals, both these terms were rejected in favour of 'Early Years Professional'. However, it is worth a closer look at the concept of the social pedagogue and the insights this may offer into the distinctiveness of the EYP role.

The role of the 'pedagogue' has its roots in nineteenth-century Germany and was developed in response to what has been termed 'schoolification', which assumes there is a bank of knowledge and skills to be acquired by a child with the teacher's role to impart these within set targets and time frameworks (Petrie, 2005). This is often referred to as the 'transmission' code of learning (Bottery, 1990) where the child is a *passive* recipient' and teacher/educator's role is that of '*active* transmitter' of knowledge. Such a model does not fit easily in an Early Years context where children are seen as developing in different ways and at different rates (DCSF, 2008a) and the adult role one of 'supporting children's learning within an enabling, facilitating and observing role rather than directly as "teachers"' (Moyles et al., 2002). Part of the definition of the pedagogue emphasises the relationship with the child as a whole being, supporting all aspects of the child's development equally and working with each child to establish positive dispositions for learning.

The concept of the pedagogue is intrinsically linked to an understanding of Early Years pedagogy. You will have the opportunity to explore this in a little more depth in Chapter 5 of this book and, indeed, there are other publications in this series (such as Allen and Whalley, 2010) which will enable you to engage with aspects of the pedagogical base for your role as EYPs. Stewart and Pugh suggest that Early Years Pedagogy is:

> *the understanding of how children learn and develop, and the practices through which we can enhance that process. It is rooted in values and beliefs about what we want for children, and supported by knowledge, theory and experience.*
>
> (Stewart and Pugh, 2007, cited in Department for
> Children Schools and Families, 2009a: 4)

The Study of Pedagogical Effectiveness in Early Learning (SPEEL) (Moyles et al., 2002) has been particularly influential in the development of the EYP role. SPEEL identified the need for highly qualified, reflective practitioners, able to demonstrate both a principled value stance and in-depth knowledge and understanding of the learning and developmental needs of young children. As you gather evidence for EYP Standards 1–6, you will need to evidence these aspects of your own role and how you are leading the practice of others.

This view of the pedagogue role and Early Years pedagogy therefore offers us a very clearly defined pattern of Early Years provision which is quite deliberately and robustly different from the school experience (Payler, 2005). Research by the British Educational Research Association Early Years Special Interest Group (BERA, 2003) suggested that pedagogical processes in the Early Years are most evident in the child's development of a sense of self and becoming sociable, in play activities (Moyles, 2005: 8 refers to 'playful pedagogy') and through the interactive nature of learning between child and adult, especially in the way that this results in shared meanings. As these processes are all central to the role of the EYP, we can begin to conclude that the concept of pedagogical leadership is one that accords with EYPS.

Boddy et al. (2005: 3) develop further understanding of the pedagogue role, describing it as one of 'strategic leadership', particularly in being reflective and applying self-knowledge to practice; being practical and creative; exercising teamwork based on dialogue, democratic practice and valuing the contribution of others; and in managing change. While some would challenge the notion that the EYP role has direct parallels with the European pedagogue (Oberhuemer, 2008), it is almost impossible not to notice some compatibility between the two roles. Look at how Sandra made the connections when she was invited on a study visit to Denmark.

CASE STUDY

Sandra, an EYP in a private setting

'Although, at first, the Denmark "pedagogue" role seemed very different to my own – and there were some noticeable differences, especially in the amount of freedom the Danes were able to give the children and the lack of emphasis on paper-based reporting – I was gradually struck by the similarities between what the pedagogue was doing and my own role. Like me, my counterpart was totally committed to the children and knew so much about them and their families. She was passionate about play-based learning – especially outdoors – and following the child's interests. I was particularly struck by the interactions between her and the children. Although I couldn't understand the actual words, I could tell from the children's responses that the conversations were helping to develop their thinking.'

REFLECTIVE TASK

Does Sandra's experience here help you to draw more parallels between the European model of the pedagogue and that of the EYP? Sandra was struck with the quality of the conversations between adult and children. How do you see this linking to S15, 16 and 26? Is there anything else from this case study that supports your reflection on your own leadership role?

Leadership of change

The concluding aspect of strategic leadership outlined by Boddy et al. (2005) is that of managing change. Rodd (2006) reminds us that change is one of the few certainties in life and that change naturally occurs in individuals, organisations and societies, with changes in any one of these necessitating change in the others. Such change is not only necessary, it is a means of creating opportunities that sustain individual and organisational survival. The task of the EYP to 'effect change' (CWDC, 2010a: 7) is a fundamental part of the rationale for the role. In Chapter 6, we examine some of the opportunities and challenges of being a 'change agent' which is an interesting concept in itself and one which actually has scientific roots in defining a catalyst or that which effects a behavioural change. Thus, the thinking behind this choice of phrase is that the EYP will intentionally or indirectly cause or accelerate changes to practice. Essentially, as an agent of change, you will need to have a high level of self-awareness, particularly in understanding your own reactions to change, and you will need emotional intelligence (Goleman, 1996). These are prerequisites to the more proactive aspects of the role as agent of change, which will include modelling appropriate behaviours and practices, sharing your knowledge and expertise with colleagues, engaging in dialogue with them, using imaginative ways of presenting new ideas and – through strong rapport – persuading them to come on board.

REFLECTIVE TASK

As you begin to explore your role as an agent of change, think about those five dimensions and see if you can identify examples from your own practice.

Table 1.2 Agents of change

Strategy for agent of change	Example from practice
Role-modelling appropriate behaviours and practices	
Sharing your knowledge and expertise	
Engaging in two-way dialogue with colleagues	
Imaginative and innovative ways to introduce change	
Persuasion	

C H A P T E R   S U M M A R Y

This book aims to support you as you prepare for the EYP validation process. In particular, it focuses on your role as leader of practice and agent of change. All of you, no matter what your route to EYPS or the type of setting you are in, should welcome the opportunity to reflect both on your own practice and on the way you lead and support others. The case studies of other EYPs or those aspiring to the role are offered in this book to help you to reflect on your own role. Different aspects of the EYP role in leading practice are explored in the remaining chapters, including that of working collaboratively with colleagues, in partnership with parents, and, in particular, contributing to multi-professional practice. In the initial research for the first edition, a tentative definition of the EYP as leader of practice emerged with the following skills, knowledge and attributes core to the role:

- reflective and reflexive practice in your own role;

- skills in decision-making;

- sound knowledge and understanding of Early Years pedagogy: the holistic needs of all children from birth to five and competence in planning, implementing and monitoring within the Early Years Foundation Stage framework (DCSF, 2008a and 2008b);

- a strong sense of the intrinsic worth of each child and all those in her/his world;

- the ability to role-model, lead and support others in high-quality practice;

- the ability to define a vision for practice within a setting;

- competence as an agent of change.

Reappraising this definition here results in rather more uncertainty than was evident when it first emerged. Perhaps what time is showing, with the diverse ways and range of roles in which EYPS is being used, is that the EYP role of leader refuses to be as rigidly defined as first thought. Despite the challenge of clear definition, however, there is now a growing understanding of the difference between 'leadership' and 'management' roles in Early Years: the manager maintains and ensures the smooth running of an organisation whereas the leader focuses on development and innovation (Solley, 2003). As you move towards EYPS, it is important that you focus your understanding on the leadership element of the role: that of leading and improving practice. In particular, you will need to demonstrate specific skills in leading EYFS provision and leading change effectively.

Moving on

In our opening discussion here on aspects of the EYP leadership role, we have identified some of the key writers on leadership in early childhood settings. In the next chapter, we engage in a review of this and other available literature on Early Years leadership. This will begin with a broad outline of some of the classic theories on leadership but will focus primarily on relevant research projects on leadership in Early Years contexts. Standards 1–6 require evidence of knowledge and understanding of principles, policy and practice. The EYP who is genuinely committed to the highest quality delivery will keep abreast of key research findings in order to consolidate, update and enhance his/her own knowledge and understanding.

PRACTICAL TASK

Table 1.3 is a series of statements made by Early Years practitioners when asked to define leadership. Please tick the judgement that most accurately fits your viewpoint.

PRACTICAL TASK CONTINUED

- *Are there any statements with which you strongly agree?*

- *Are there any with which you strongly disagree?*

- *Your judgements are based to a large extent on your own professional values. Are you aware of how these have been shaped?*

Table 1.3 Defining leadership

An effective leader is:	Strongly agree	Agree	Neither agree nor disagree	Disagree	Strongly disagree
1. highly qualified					
2. someone who commands respect					
3. someone who is easy to relate to					
4. someone who models good practice					
5. able to identify creative solutions					
6. able to acknowledge her/his own vulnerabilities and mistakes					
7. skilled in conflict management					
8. able to relate to a wide range of people					
9. child-centred in her/his practice					
10. respecting and valuing of all members of the team					
11. able to steer change in practice					
12. able to delegate					

Self-assessment questions

1. What are the main differences between 'leadership' and 'management' as defined by Law and Glover? (Answer: page 3)

2. Why was the NPQICL developed? How is this route qualitatively different from that taken by EYPS candidates? (Answer: pages 1–2, 5)

3. Name the four aspects of leadership 'behaviour' that Rodd (2006) has identified. (Answer: page 7)

4. What are the four 'branches' of Moyles' (2006) Effective Management and Leadership Scheme? (Answer: page 7)

5. In what ways does the Early Years Professional role mirror the European model of 'social pedagogue'? (Answer – see definition on page 10)

Moyles, J. (2006) The leadership qualities branch, Chapter 3 in *Effective Leadership and Management in the Early Years.* Maidenhead: Open University Press.

Rodd, J. (2006) Unpacking leadership in the early childhood context, Chapter 1 in *Leadership in Early Childhood.* Maidenhead: Open University Press.

2 Leadership in the Early Years: a review of the literature

CHAPTER   OBJECTIVES

This chapter provides a review of current literature relating to leadership theories and research findings. Starting with broad reference to classic leadership theories, the focus will narrow to consider further the literature on leadership in the Early Years. Drawing on both UK-based and international research, including Scandinavia, the USA, Australia and New Zealand, you will have opportunity to see how our emerging definition of leadership of practice has been influenced from a number of sources. As an Early Years Professional, you are expected to have graduate level knowledge and understanding of the principles that underpin quality practice. The reflective tasks in this chapter will support the application of this knowledge to your own practice and in the way you lead the practice of others.

After reading this chapter you should be able to:
- understand some of the classic leadership theories;
- discuss how these have been applied to research studies on leadership in the Early Years;
- reflect on how these might shape our understanding of leadership of practice in the Early Years;
- apply some of the insights from theory and research to your own practice.

This chapter is wide-ranging and will help you to reflect on how you influence and lead the practice of others in relation to a number of the Standards for Early Years Professionals, particularly S1–6.

Introduction

The history of all cultures is punctuated with the names of great leaders and there have always been particular people whom others will follow (Doyle and Smith, 1999): Mahatma Gandhi, Joan of Arc, Winston Churchill, and American Indian Chief Sitting Bull are but a few, for the list is endless. But we need to ask two questions: firstly, what makes them 'great' and secondly, is 'great' always 'good'? When we think of leaders like Adolf Hitler and others who have led with a dictatorial style, we recognise that not all leadership has beneficial outcomes. Are good leaders born or can they be 'made'/trained? Although you will encounter much theory in this chapter, you should try to keep the focus on your own leadership opportunities and in particular consider the particular context in which you work and your role as leader of practice.

Think again about the task in Chapter 1 about what makes a 'good leader'. Can you continue to identify the particular characteristics that make a leader worthy of following? What are the traits or qualities that you associate with a 'good leader'?

Theories of leadership

Numerous books have been written which focus on the development of our theoretical understanding of leadership (Yukl, 1989; Clark and Clark, 1990; Bass and Stogdill, 1990). Most of these belong more appropriately to the world of finance, commerce, politics and business. However, it is worth considering briefly those that have emerged as *classic* theories or models of leadership (Doyle and Smith, 1999). As you consider these, it will be helpful to think back to your own experience of being led and to your current experiences of leading practice. Is there any particular model which 'speaks to' or resonates with your situation?

We have already identified that an absolute definition of leadership is hard to find. However, we have stated that in the context of EYPS, leadership is usually linked to the concept of the 'leader'. If we assume this, four key themes stand out:

1. to lead involves influencing the behaviour of others;

2. where there are leaders there are followers;

3. leaders seem to come to the fore when there is a crisis or special problem. In other words, they often become visible when an innovative response is needed;

4. our expectation is that leaders are people who have a clear idea of what they want to achieve and why.

Thus, good leaders are generally thought to be people who are able to think and act creatively in routine and non-routine situations and who set out to influence the actions, beliefs and feelings of others (Doyle and Smith, 1999).

Over the past few decades, there have been four main 'generations' of leadership theory:

• trait theories;

• behavioural theories;

• situational or contingency theories;

• transformational theories.

As van Maurik (2001) has pointed out, it is important to recognise that the four 'generations' are not mutually exclusive or totally time-bound but each has something to contribute to our overall understanding of leadership theory.

Trait theories

What is it that makes someone exceptional in this respect? The people in history who have been labelled great leaders have very different qualities. Bennis (1998) suggests that strong leaders know what they want, why they want it and how to communicate this to others in order to gain cooperation. Early trait research by Stogdill (1948), Mann (1959) and others suggested that there might be personality characteristics that appear to differentiate leaders from followers. Later work (such as Wright, 1996) refutes this and has found no differences between leaders and followers with respect to these characteristics and even found some evidence that people who possessed them were *less* likely to become leaders. Nevertheless, many of the popular books on the subject today still include a list of traits that are thought to be central to effective leadership. Gardner's (1989) study of North American organisations and leaders produced a list of traits or attributes for effective leadership that included physical vitality and stamina, intelligence and action-oriented judgement, task competence, the capacity to motivate people, trustworthiness and decisiveness.

A later study in the UK (Horne and Stedman Jones, 2001) identified the following key characteristics that leaders of organisations should possess: knowledge, inspiration, strategic thinking, a sense of vision and courage. One of the issues often raised about trait theories concerns their apparent 'maleness' (Rosener, 1997; Rodd, 2006). When men and women are asked about each other's characteristics and leadership qualities, some significant patterns emerge. Both tend to have difficulties in seeing women as leaders. Indeed, the attributes on these lists are often viewed as male and this has particular relevance to Early Years practice with its predominantly female workforce. Rodd (2006) offers a useful critique of leadership and gender. While there is risk of over-simplification, she argues that the traditional model of leadership is considered to be more male in orientation and is dominated by control, power, domination and competition and this is one reason why, within Early Years, women have generally been reluctant to assert themselves as 'leaders'. Grant (cited in Rodd, 2006) believes that the new prevailing model for leadership is actually female, with the focus more on relationships, consensus, collaboration and flexibility.

CASE STUDY

Ken *is a popular leader of the pre-school room in a children's centre, with a collaborative style of working. He exhibits none of the 'traditional male attributes' described above. Indeed, his female colleagues all consider him 'one of them' and there is generally very effective teamwork in the base room.*

Linda, *by contrast, is the supervisor of a pre-school group in her local village. She has worked in the setting for 18 years and is a forceful character who has definite ideas about how the group should be organised and run and who adopts a fairly authoritarian style with her staff. The management committee, mainly parents, are very much in awe of her and generally allow her to have her way.*

We need to guard against gender stereotyping leadership traits but do you think trait theories show bias to 'maleness'?

What has been the impact of this on Early Years practice?

Are you aware of this in your own experience?

More importantly – can you identify core leadership traits that transcend gender?

Behavioural theories

Many of the attributes listed by Gardner (1989) are, in fact, *behaviours.* This was a natural development of leadership theory: a move towards what leaders do, rather than the qualities they demonstrate. This became very much the way of understanding leadership during the 1960s. Different patterns of behaviour were grouped together and labelled as leadership 'styles'. The most notable product of the approach was Blake and Mouton's Managerial Grid, which identified four main styles of leadership: *concern for task*, where the leader looks for high levels of productivity in order to achieve objectives; concern *for people,* where the needs of individuals are given high priority; *directive leadership*, where leaders take decisions for others; *and participative leadership*, where there is a shared decision-making process (Blake and Mouton, 1964, cited in Wright, 1996: 36–37)

Increasingly, limitations on this behavioural approach were identified (McGregor, 1970) and later studies (Sadler, 1997) suggested that it was difficult to state categorically that style of leadership was significant in determining whether it was successful or not. In fact, neither trait nor behavioural theories take sufficient account of the *context* in which leadership takes place. The style and behaviour of leaders are affected considerably by those they are working with and the environment in which they are working.

REFLECTIVE TASK

Consider the four types of leadership behaviours summarised by Wright (1996) above. Do any of these resonate with your experience of being 'led' in the past? Think particularly of Wright's concept of 'participative leadership' and how this links to the core skill of the EYP role in leading and supporting others.

Situational or contingency theories

Given the limitations of trait and behavioural theories of leadership, researchers began to focus on the *contexts* in which leadership is exercised, with the ensuing notion that there are a number of variables to be considered. Various views emerged, the most extreme being that just about everything was determined by the contexts, while style and behaviour counted for virtually nothing. However, most writers brought the idea of style with them, believing that particular contexts would demand particular forms of leadership. Thus, the key to effective leadership is seen to be the ability to work in different ways, to change the style to suit the situation. Can you see that this might have particular relevance for the EYP role as leader of practice?

Developing from situational theories of leadership, a *contingency* approach began to emerge. For instance, Fiedler and Garcia (1987) argued that effectiveness depends on two interacting factors: leadership style and the degree to which the situation gives the leader control and influence. They described three things as important here:

- the relationship between the leaders and followers: if leaders are liked and respected they are more likely to have the support of others;

- the structure of the task: if the task is clearly spelled out as to goals, methods and standards of performance then it is more likely that leaders will be able to exert influence;

- position power: if an organisation or group confers powers on the leader for the purpose of getting the job done, then this may well increase the influence of the leader.

(Adapted from Fiedler and Garcia, 1987: 51–67)

Leadership and the cultural context

We have already noted the importance of guarding against gender stereotyping in any discussion on leadership. Indeed, any contrasts between the styles of men and women may be down to the situation and culture. In management, for example, women are more likely to be in positions of authority in people-oriented sectors such as personnel management, so this more nurturing style is likely to be emphasised. It should also be noted that most of the theorists/writers identified so far are from North America and the issue of cultural bias must be acknowledged. There is a great deal of evidence to suggest that cultural factors influence the way that people carry out, and respond to, different leadership styles. For example, some cultures are more individualistic, or value family as against bureaucratic models, or have very different expectations about how people address and talk to each other. Chakraborty's study (2003) suggests that leadership in the East is dominantly 'feminist-intuitive' whereas that in the West is 'masculine-rational'.

REFLECTIVE TASK

How important do you think the 'context' of leadership is? What contextual factors can you identify that facilitate your ability to lead practice effectively in your setting? Are there any hindering factors?

Transformational theories

Transforming leaders are visionary leaders who seek to appeal to their followers' 'better nature and move them toward higher and more universal needs and purposes' (Bolman and Deal, 1997: 314). In other words, the leader is seen as a change agent. It is this model that has particular relevance for you as you seek to demonstrate your EYP skills as a leader of change.

Bass (1985) believes the transformational leader can:

- raise our level of awareness and our level of consciousness about the significance and value of designated outcomes, and ways of reaching them;

- get us to transcend our own self-interest for the sake of the team, organisation or larger polity;

- alter our need level (after Maslow, 1986);

- expand our range of wants and needs.

(Based on Bass, 1985; Wright, 1996)

The EYP role is seen as key to transforming practice, so the concept of transformational leadership is one to take seriously.

REFLECTIVE TASK

Look again at Bass's understanding of the transformational leader.

Think about a specific colleague whose practice you are aiming to lead and support? Substitute the name of that colleague as in the example below and think how you are able to exercise leadership in this transformational way.

1. How am I raising M's awareness and levels of consciousness about the significance of what we are trying to achieve in our setting and the value of achieving our goals?
2. How am I supporting M in rising above self-interest and seeing the 'bigger picture' for the sake of the children and setting?
3. How can I work with M so that she herself wants to see and understand her role differently?

Alongside the classic theories that underpin our comprehension of leadership, there are three main groups of writers who have helped inform and shape contemporary understanding. There are those who emphasise the team dimension of leadership and the role of team leader – such as Belbin (1993). Then there are those who describe the leader as a catalyst of change, such as Bennis (1998) and Covey (1989). Finally, there are those who see the leader as strategic visionary, such as Senge (1994). These three aspects of leadership are interconnecting and equally important.

While we remain in the broad arena of classic leadership theories, two further concepts are considered: those relating to *authority* and *charisma*. Authority within organisations is usually viewed as 'the possession of powers based on a formal role' (Heifetz, 1994). This is how you might see your line manager. Do leaders have the same power? Doyle and Smith (1999) suggest that where leaders have the power to sack, demote or disadvantage, this may well result in compliance but not necessarily respect. They argue that the authority of the leader is rather more subtle and includes the ability to deal with crises and to manage change without being fazed by any challenges or obstacles. Leaders may have formal authority, but rely to a large extent on informal authority and influence, which

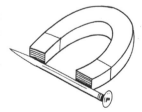

flows from their personal qualities and actions and generates the respect of their peers. The EYP is likely to have informal, rather than formal, authority and influence and this can be an advantage in leading practice. The leader then has greater freedom of movement and more choice to focus on specific areas of responsibility (for the EYP this is, of course, 'practice') rather than having responsibility for the maintenance of a whole organisation (Doyle and Smith, 1999).

The concept of the *charisma* of the leader has been central to Western understanding of leadership. The literal meaning of the word is 'a gift of grace, or of God' (Wright, 1996: 194) but its meaning in use is very difficult to articulate – although most people have a good inner sense of what constitutes a charismatic leader. When discussing charisma, we are in the arena of traits and qualities once more: the charismatic leader has particular skills, personality and presence. However, this is only one side of the notion of charisma and it is equally important to explore the situations or contexts in which charisma manifests itself. In times of distress – personally, within families, organisations and nationally – there is a tendency to seek figures who provide answers and demonstrate strength of purpose. Think of the role of Winston Churchill in the Second World War or Martin Luther King fighting against racial injustice in the southern states of the USA. In these examples, the emergence of the charismatic leader is interactional, that is it originates from a collective need for one to lead within a particular context.

The role of the charismatic leader, however, can also include heavy dependency. It can mean the loss of individual autonomy and relinquishing responsibility. Such leaders can be placed on an impossible pedestal and a huge gulf can grow between 'me' and 'him/her'. It can create a sense of invincibility and power in the leader and a corresponding sense of powerlessness in those who are led. It can also lead to significant conflict when the tide turns against the charismatic leader. In the following case study, a charismatic new manager has just been appointed in a private setting.

CASE STUDY

Adrienne is appointed as the new manager of a private day nursery. She arrives with extensive experience in Early Years in schools and has also worked in South America as an Early Years teacher in a charity project for street children. The nursery has just had a poor Ofsted report but Adrienne approaches this as a challenging opportunity, not simply a concern. She is highly energetic, has huge self-confidence, is striking to look at with her jet-black long curly hair and has a very positive disposition. Very quickly, the whole nursery staff warms to her; the children love her, the parents engage well with her and she always has lots to share with staff in the weekly staff meetings. Moreover, Adrienne spends as much time as she can in the various base rooms, modelling new approaches to practice to the staff team. Very quickly, there are significant changes to many aspects of practice across the nursery.

REFLECTIVE TASK

- *In what ways has Adrienne used authority and charisma effectively here?*
- *In what ways does Adrienne exemplify effective leadership?*
- *What are the potential pitfalls?*

We have outlined here some of the main theoretical frameworks that inform our understanding of leadership. You might have observed that such frameworks sit more comfortably with the forms of leadership required for business, the armed forces, government and so on. Possibly the two areas of leadership practice that are most closely related to that within the EYP role are school and integrated centre leadership/management. However, the emphasis of roles and responsibilities identified for school and children centre leaders is principally that of providing strategic direction, managing team work, networking and collaboration with other settings and professionals, managing operations and accountability (DfES/Price Waterhouse Coopers, 2007). While there are some similarities between the EYP role and that of the integrated centre's leader – such as the close observation of individual children – the EYP role carries none of the 'management of an organisation' element that is so core to that of a headteacher in school or an integrated centre leader.

In Chapter 1, we identified some general confusion in distinguishing the role of 'leader' from that of 'manager'. The EYP role is clearly that of the 'leader' – but of practice and not an organisation. It is helpful, therefore, to consider now some of the key writers and research studies in the field of early childhood leadership. Historically, much of these precede the introduction of the EYP role but all offer some insights into issues that relate specifically to the complex field of leadership in Early Years settings, with some of the later studies offering initial critique of the EYP role itself.

Leadership in the Early Years

Smith and Langston's work (1999) is one the key texts to be referenced in any review of leadership in the Early Years. Although the focus of their work is on managing staff, their writing is particularly helpful in clarifying distinctions between leadership and management roles. In particular, they describe how the behaviour of the leader/manager can result in ineffective teamwork. Drawing on earlier work (Shea, 1993; Bryman, 1986), Smith and Langston offer a self-appraisal tool whereby leaders can identify current behaviours within their role and also reflect on what would be preferable behaviours.

Especially linked to standards 1–6

Table 2.1 shows the leadership behaviours identified by Smith and Langston (1999: 11–12). Reflect on the way you demonstrate leadership in your setting and illustrate with an example from practice.

Table 2.1 Leadership behaviours

Leadership behaviour:	Example from practice:
Inspires	
Thinks	
Motivates	
Initiates change	
Dictates	
Takes decisions	
Sets objectives	
Sets the pace	
Inspires loyalty	
Self-sufficient	

Jillian Rodd (1996, 1997, 2006) has made a major contribution to our understanding of leadership in the Early Years and, indeed, is highly respected internationally. She writes from the perspective of over 30 years' experience and research in the early childhood field and has listened to and consulted widely with practitioners in all sectors, with parents, school staff, academic educators and policy makers. Clearly, Rodd's contribution to shaping and informing our understanding of the nature of leadership in the Early Years and its impact on professionalism in the field is hugely significant.

Rodd has also contributed to the bank of emerging global research evidence relating to leadership in the Early Years but is one of many to highlight that it is only since 2000 that research in this area has expanded (Muijs et al., 2004; Dunlop, 2008). Like Sylva et al. (1999) and others, Rodd strongly believes the evidence of a clear link between effective leadership and organisational performance. However, in her own 1997 study of 79 managers in Early Years settings, Rodd found that there was far more emphasis on maintenance (i.e. management) of an organisation than on development (i.e. leadership) though there was consensus among all the participants that they needed further training (preferably in-service) on the leadership aspects of their role. In Chapter 1, you were introduced to the work of Janet Moyles, whose research led to the development of the Effective Leadership and Management Scheme for Early Years (ELMS-EY) (Moyles, 2006). The ELMS-EY was introduced in direct response to the lack of training opportunities available to those who lead and manage Early Years settings and identifies skills, qualities, attributes, characteristics and attitudes which Moyles believes are necessary for the overall roles of leadership and management.

CASE STUDY

Marge, 44, has worked as an Early Years practitioner since she was 18 and, for the last seven years has been manager of a 68-place full-day care setting. Marge is outgoing, confident and competent in her role in maintaining the smooth running of the nursery. There is a low staff turnover and a healthy waiting list. Marge has continued to progress academically and has recently achieved an early childhood studies degree. As she prepares for EYPS, she finds herself reflecting on differences between her role as manager and leader in the setting.

Khalid, 35, has a fine arts degree and for some years worked as an illustrator of children's books (which he continues to do freelance). When he was 33, he decided he wanted to work directly with children and was accepted as a Full EYPS pathway candidate, with placements first in a children's centre and then in a suburban voluntary pre-school setting. Last year, he became the joint leader of the pre-school and is already strongly influencing the children's opportunities for artistic expression. Khalid feels he had to 'do' leadership very quickly on this pathway but now finds himself reflecting on 'what makes an effective leader'.

REFLECTIVE TASK

1. *Marge and Khalid are both reflecting on their roles as 'leaders'. What do you think their respective training needs are here? How do these differ?*

2. *Think about the opportunities you have to reflect on your leadership role. What other training might you find helpful?*

Leadership for learning

In Chapter 1, we considered some recent work by Siraj-Blatchford and Manni (2007) which builds on earlier studies, in particular *Researching Effective Pedagogy in the Early Years (REPEY)* (Siraj-Blatchford et al., 2002) and *Effective Provision of Pre-school Education (EPPE)* (Sylva et al., 2004). These two studies combine to create a representative picture of pre-school effectiveness and identify a clear correlation between 'strong leadership' (particularly where some of the staff are graduates or teacher-trained) and 'children's progress' (Siraj-Blatchford and Manni, 2007: 1). Children's progress is also linked to adults who have a good understanding of 'appropriate pedagogical content' and the pedagogue role. These studies have further strengthened our understanding and expectations of the EYP role.

The Effective Leadership in the Early Years (ELEYS) project (Siraj-Blatchford and Manni, 2007) was developed in response to the ongoing investment in the Children's Workforce.

Between 1997 and 2010, the government invested around £2 billion in pre-school education and recognised that such investment requires skilled leadership. Siraj-Blatchford and Manni (2007: 1) ask: 'Where is the firm evidence regarding the characteristics of effective leadership in Early Years settings?' It is this question which the ELEYS study seeks to address. Drawing on some of the insights from classical leadership theory, they conclude that the role of leadership in the Early Years is essentially that of 'leadership for learning' (Siraj-Blatchford and Manni, 2007: 12) where the fundamental requirements for the role are as follows:

- **contextual literacy** – situational leadership; consideration of the situation in which the leader operates and the people s/he is leading;

- **a commitment to collaboration** – where effective pedagogic and parental support are complementary and where there are positive inter-agency partnerships;

- **a commitment to the improvement of outcomes for all children** – where children's development is considered holistically and where individual needs are identified and met.

REFLECTIVE TASK

Can you link these elements of the leadership role identified by Siraj-Blatchford and Manni (2007) to the EYP Standards? Focus particularly, though not exclusively, on Standards 1–6.

Although Rodd, Moyles and Siraj-Blatchford are based mainly in the UK, they have all gained international respect and draw widely on insights and studies from other parts of the world. A review by Dunlop (2008) of the available literature on leadership in the Early Years offers a succinct summary of much of the relevant research since 2000 which recognises the contribution of Rodd, Moyles and Siraj-Blatchford, among others. A number of key themes emerge from this review which can be usefully explored in any reflection on the EYP role and you are encouraged to think about the application of some of these to your own work and practice.

How important is leadership in the Early Years?

As in the UK, since the late 1990s, early education and care have received unparalleled political attention in many countries. Dunlop's review (2008: 27) suggests a clear case for a 'relationship between appropriate leadership in Early Years services and the effectiveness of those services'. This confirms the findings of the EPPE Project (Sylva et al., 2004) while studies from the US 'Head Start' Programme show that competent and stable leadership is essential to the effectiveness of programme implementation (Ramey et al., 2000).

What are the main roles of leaders in the Early Years?

Dunlop suggests that what emerge from her review are different understandings of how leadership is viewed in various types of early childhood settings. Indeed, in an earlier review of the available literature on leadership in early childhood, Muijs et al. (2004: 161) concluded that the overwhelming picture to emerge is that leaders in early childhood settings have a 'multiplicity of roles which are context specific'. A study in Finland (Hujala, 2004) suggests that, within the Scandinavian context, early childhood leadership is determined to a large extent by factors specific to a particular setting, such as the way the leader sees the role and the way s/he is viewed within the community. One recent view of leadership is that it is not an isolated activity invested in a single person but, rather, 'a variety of people contribute to effective leadership and that leadership, is, therefore distributed' (Dunlop, 2008: 4). This notion of 'distributed leadership' is based on Spillane et al.'s (2004) work and has been promoted as a paradigm for school leadership. However, caution is needed here. While the notion of distributed leadership might well connect to practice in the Early Years, what does emerge clearly in the Dunlop review, particularly from countries where state provision of early childhood services is still relatively new – New Zealand, for example – is the need for a distinctive understanding of Early Years leadership, which is quite different from that required in schools and other settings (Thornton, 2005). Certainly, the available research studies show leadership in early childhood to be very complex with the need for 'role clarity towards effective leadership . . . an area for development' (Dunlop, 2008: 28). While the Dunlop review addresses early childhood leadership in its wider sense, perhaps we can see here some explanation why any crisp definition of the EYP role as 'leader of practice' is so hard to find!

What are the characteristics of effective leaders in the Early Years?

While identifying major weaknesses in the research base in this area, Dunlop does draw on work by Yukl and Chavez (2002) which suggests that the most influential approaches to Early Years leadership include: rational persuasion; consultation; collaboration; and inspirational appeal. Dunlop also cites work by Bloom (2000) which concludes that early childhood leaders need to demonstrate competence in three areas which include those specifically relating to early childhood and to broader leadership:

- *knowledge* – including child development, pedagogical strategies, group dynamics and organisational theory;
- *skills* – including technical, human and conceptual skills (e.g. budgeting); and
- *attitudes* – including a sense of moral purpose.

How much professional development and training is there for leaders in the Early Years?

Training is essential to provide the relevant knowledge and skills for leadership roles in Early Years (Dunlop, 2002; Sylva et al., 2002). Muijs et al. (2004) believed the lack of training up to 2000 indicated the generally low status of the early childhood context. Historically, training had not been deemed necessary. Arguably, the situation is changing and, as Dunlop (2008: 20) identifies: 'where training is provided, effects appear positive'. She cites one example at Pen Green where Margy Whalley's team is leading on the NPQICL (Whalley et al., 2005). Indeed, the development of EYPS and the training and preparation pathways that have been established to enable the achievement of EYPS can, themselves, be viewed indicative of a response, at government level. Although the model for EYP as leader of practice is distinctively different from that offered in the NPQICL role, there are shared principles here, such as:

- establishing links between leadership and learning;

- focusing on task and process;

- focusing on practitioner research;

- keeping a reflective journal;

- exploration of the dynamic between theory and practice.

(Based on Whalley, 2005b)

REFLECTIVE TASK

From this summary of key research data since 2000, what strikes you as relevant to your role as an EYP? In particular, look at the knowledge, skills and attitudes suggested by Bloom (2000) as necessary for competent leaders. Can you make links with the EYP Standards here?

C H A P T E R   S U M M A R Y

In this chapter, we have once again acknowledged the influence of key writers in the field of leadership in the Early Years. We have reviewed much of the recent literature and you have had the opportunity to begin to apply some of the key insights from it to your own role as a leader of practice. There is scope for much more high-quality research on leadership in early childhood. From the research studies that do exist, there is clear evidence about the importance of the leadership role, the complexity of its function and the need for more specific training programmes and professional development. Since the publication of the Dunlop review (2008) there have been other studies which are stimulating and contributing to ongoing discourse about the EYP role. Miller (2008) offers a critical review of policy development which has led to the creation of the EYP role. A small-scale study by Lloyd and Hallet (2010: 19) suggests a high level of 'commitment to professional practice, leadership and professional ideals among Early Years practitioners working as EYPs or studying on . . . one of the . . . pathways' but concludes that the professionalisation of the Early Years workforce is still 'a work in progress'. Similarly, Simpson (2010) draws on data from interviews with a small number of EYPs who were amongst the first in the country to achieve the status, and concludes that EYPs themselves need greater autonomy in defining the professional aspects to the role. Clearly, as you seek to identify opportunities in your own practice to demonstrate your competence as a leader of practice, you will be contributing to a wider canvas of understanding of this crucial role.

Moving on

As EYPs, one of your key roles is to lead others in creating an inclusive and anti-discriminatory ethos in your setting. In the next chapter, the focus moves towards the child/ren in the setting and their families and confirms the importance of the *context* of leadership. You will have further opportunity to think of the families represented in your setting and the community in which you work. If you have attended any relevant in-service training or professional development opportunities on equality practice, re-read your notes and reflect especially on your key role in cascading information to colleagues and leading change.

FURTHER READING

Dunlop, A.-W. (2008) A Literature Review on Leadership in the Early Years. Available at www.ltscotland. org.uk/Images/leadershipreview_tcm4-499140.doc

Siraj-Blatchford, I. and Manni, L. (2007) *Effective Leadership in the Early Years Sector: The ELEYS Study*. London: The Institute of Education, University of London. Available at: http://www.gtce.org.uk/ shared/contentlibs/126795/93128/120213/eleys_study.pdf

3 Leadership of equality practice

CHAPTER OBJECTIVES

In this chapter, the focus moves to leadership of inclusive practice and the role of the leader in identifying and challenging anti-discriminatory practice. Definitions are explored and relevant legislation and statutory frameworks are outlined as we consider how the leader of practice should act as a role model in promoting appropriate values and principles – so central to the Early Years Foundation Stage framework. The role of the leader as one who 'creates a community', embracing diversity, is explored and, through case studies and other tasks, there are opportunities for reflection on the opportunities and challenges for leadership of practice.

After reading this chapter you should be able to:
- reflect on how you model and promote appropriate values and principles relating to equality;
- appraise critically how you identify and respond to the needs of each unique child;
- apply an appropriate understanding of how you can lead and support equality practice in your setting especially in dealing with discriminatory practices.

This chapter focuses particularly on Standards 2, 4, 12, 18, 23

Introduction

Good practice for equality is partly a focus on the individual children and families in your setting . . . But also covers the image of the world that you are giving children: the big picture that extends beyond their own back yard.

(Lindon, 2006: 3)

In the previous chapter, we saw that there was much emphasis on the importance of the *situational* nature of leadership, particularly in the theories of Fiedler and Garcia (1987) and Moyles (2006). Siraj-Blatchford and Manni (2007: 12) refer to this as 'contextual literacy' and describe it as situational leadership where the leader is totally conversant with the particular context in which s/he operates and the people s/he is leading.

In carrying out your leadership role as an EYP, it is important that you engage whole-heartedly with the particular context in which you are working as a leader of practice. This includes knowledge and understanding about the children and their families, the staff in the setting and wider knowledge of the local community. In turn, the 'local' needs to be seen in the framework of the wider national and even international context.

In this chapter, we start by defining what we mean by 'equality practice' and reflect on where we have come from in our understanding of the concept, starting with a brief review of relevant legislation and critical issues in Early Years practice. We then focus on current challenges and opportunities and ask questions about how we can best take equality practice forward into the future. You will be encouraged to consider how you can best develop innovative ideas for the individual child and motivate and support others in their practice.

The legislative framework

One of the four key themes in the framework for the Early Years Foundation Stage (EYFS) (DCSF, 2008a) is that of 'the unique child' with a stated commitment that diversity of individuals and communities is valued and respected and no child or family is discriminated against.

Indeed, this chapter might have been more appropriately entitled 'leadership for the needs of the unique child' as we intend to identify many factors that need to be taken into account in building up a bank of knowledge and understanding about each individual as we work towards '"equalising" opportunities for those children and families whose situation or group identity may place them at a disadvantage' (Lindon, 2006: 3).

REFLECTIVE TASK

Think of recognisable attributes that help us identify each child's uniqueness: gender; ability; age/stage of development; ethnicity; culture; religion; language; socio-economic factors; in-child factors (personality, learning preferences, etc.).

- *Are there any other factors you think should be added here?*

- *How do you lead others to gather essential information about a new child coming into your setting?*

- *How is this information shared on a 'need to know' basis with other team members? What is your role as leader of practice in this?*

There are many complex issues relating to equality practice, most of which are beyond the parameters of the present discussion. At risk of over-simplification of these issues, a précis of the past fifty years or so in the UK suggests that we have slowly moved from a position where disadvantaged or different families are viewed as a 'problem' to seeking their integration into the 'mainstream' of society. From the 1980s onwards, legislative changes and increasing social awareness have led to a celebration of diversity. Initially legislation relating to equality focused on identifying discriminatory actions and making these unlawful. Gradually, there has been a shift in emphasis to placing an active duty on promoting equality. As EYPs, you have a professional responsibility to understand something of our social history, of the key changes in the law and how these have informed and shaped policy and practice in the Early Years.

Look at the following list relating to equality law and other legislation concerning the welfare of children. An internet search for sites such as www.equalityhumanrights.com will enable you to find out more about any of these. What is the main impact on Early Years provision/practice of each of these pieces of legislation? How do these affect your role? Note down your answers:

- *Equal Pay Act (1970)*
- *Sexual Discrimination Act (1975)*
- *Race Relations Act (1976) with Amendment Act (2000)*
- *Disability Discrimination Act (1995)*
- *Special Educational Needs and Disability Act (2001)*
- *Equality Acts 2006, 2010*
- *Children Acts 1989, 2004*
- *1989 United Nations Convention on the Rights of the Child – especially Articles 2, 14, 20 and 30.*

(Childcare Act, 2006)

Dickins (2002) believes that equality of opportunity has always been given prominence in Early Years practice but the direction of travel of policy and legislation over the past two decades has encouraged and consolidated this. Particularly influential here have been the Children Act 1989, the Rumbold Report (DES, 1990), *Curriculum Guidance for the Foundation Stage* (QCA, 2000), the *Birth to Three Matters* framework (DfES, 2002) and the National Standards set to regulate childcare provision (DfES, 2001). Commitment to meeting the needs of all children and improving outcomes for them is central to the Early Years Foundation Stage framework (DCSF, 2008a) and enshrined in the Childcare Act 2006. EYP Standards 2, 4, 12, 18 and 23 remind you that this is a critical part of your role as leader of practice and recently published guidance is signposted at the end of the chapter to support you in this aspect of your role.

The words and language we use are of enormous importance in any consideration of equality practice. First of all there is the need for precision of language, as there are a number of terms relating to equality practice and definitions are not always firmly agreed. Secondly, the EYP has a responsibility to observe reactions to spoken and non-verbal language and, where necessary, adjust these in the light of these reactions even if there is no deliberate intention of excluding any individual or being impolite. Lindon (2006) offers a very useful list of definitions and these are used here for clarity:

- **Equality Practice:** a move towards the common ground for different group identities, treating each with equal concern and responding specifically to any needs identified.
- **Promoting Equality/Equal Opportunities:** actions integral to regular practice in order to ensure that all children are enabled to have positive experiences supporting personal identity.

- **Anti-Discriminatory Practice:** an active attempt (where practitioners take the initiative) to promote positive attitudes and behaviour, to challenge and change negative outlooks and actions on the basis of any group identity.

- **Anti-Bias Practice or Curriculum:** a framework of activities, play materials and experiences that avoid unnecessary stereotypes and actively promote understanding and knowledge of all groups within society.

- **Inclusion:** this term, along with an **inclusive approach** was initially developed with reference to disability. These terms, and also the concept of **social inclusion**, are now generally applied to practice about equality. In essence, it means an active effort to address ways in which children or adults may be excluded – intentionally or unintentionally – from services or experiences.

(Adapted from Lindon, 2006: 13)

REFLECTIVE TASK

Read and re-read Lindon's definitions above and think how these relate to Standards 2, 4, 12, 18, 23 in particular. From your own role, identify three examples of proactive responses related to equality practice which you have undertaken and show how you have supported others in equality practice.

Early Years Foundation Stage

The Statutory Framework for the EYFS (DCSF, 2008a) sets out the responsibilities of providers for equality practice very clearly.

Providers have a responsibility to ensure positive attitudes to diversity and difference – not only so that every child is included and not disadvantaged, but also so that they can learn from the earliest age to value diversity in others and grow up making a positive contribution to society. Practitioners should focus on each child's individual learning, development and care needs by:

- *Removing or helping to overcome barriers for children where these already exist.*

- *Being alert to the early signs of needs that could lead to later difficulties and responding quickly and appropriately, involving other agencies as necessary.*

- *Stretching and challenging all children.*

(DCSF, 2008a: 1.14)

All registered settings for children from birth to five are now required to demonstrate compliance with this statutory framework and most do this through written policy statements which may be called 'Equality of Opportunity', 'Special Educational Needs (SEN) ' or 'Inclusion' policies, or a combination of these. All settings are required to have a designated member of staff in the role of Special Educational Needs Coordinator (SENCO) and some settings also have a designated Equality or Inclusion Coordinator. These policies require revision and rethinking on a regular basis.

Policy in action

Law, policy and rhetoric are all very well. The challenge for us all lies in translating the above into everyday good, reflective practice which demonstrates total commitment to the underpinning ethos and meaning of them.

> *Effective policy making is an active and dynamic process that ideally involves all the stakeholder groups including parents and children at some level.*
>
> (Dickins, 2002: 19)

Prescriptive or ready-made policies have their place but the most effective policies are ones where there is shared ownership and understanding of the contents. Only then can they be applied effectively. Dickins (2002) suggests that policy-making is an active and dynamic process which should involve all stakeholders, including parents and children, at some level. Skills in developing policies should be viewed as fundamental to the role of the EYP. A policy is a statement of intentions for your setting and should draw on the key principles and values that inform and guide your work and then identify a strategy of how these are put into practice. Your role as leader of practice may well include writing policy documents. Think about the following sections:

- key intentions, values or principles that guide practice;

- the general environment – accessibility, relevance, stimulation, safety, etc.;

- the curriculum and programme of activities;

- parent/family involvement;

- staff training, development and support;

- roles and responsibilities of key individuals – such as key persons, SENCO, Inclusion Coordinator, etc.;

- monitoring policy implementation;

- timetables for implementation;

- publicity and dissemination policy;

- timetable for evaluation and review of policy.

(Based on Dickins, 2002; Lindon, 2006)

Almost certainly you will have at least one written policy statement relating to equality practice in your setting. Use the following questions to appraise the effectiveness of this at the present time.

PRACTICAL TASK

1. What current examples of equality practice involving children and families from your setting can you use to demonstrate that your policy/policies is/are working in an active way?

---

2. *Are the details of the policy/policies clear to you and everyone in the team? What evidence do you have to support this?*

3. *Are the details of the policy/policies clear to the families in your setting? What measures do you have in place to ensure policies are accessible to all families? Do systems exist to regularly review how policy information is shared with all families?*

4. *How confident are you to share your practice with other professionals and, if necessary, how would you/could you challenge advice that may conflict with your own principles for good practice?*

5. *How have you personally accessed and used opportunities for recent professional development in this area?*

6. *What are your information systems for ensuring that you are up to date with any changes in local or national guidance or how the law could affect your practice and setting?*

7. *In what ways have you led and supported others in your setting in equality practice?*

(Based on Lindon, 2006)

Personal value stance

One of the most important ways you will demonstrate leadership of equality practice is through your personal value stance. If you are able to lead by example with a genuinely positive attitude to equality practice and a willingness to learn more and to reflect regularly on your understanding, this will make a vital difference to the ethos of your setting. Again, this is a complex area but as a reflective EYP, you need to be aware of your own personal and professional journey and particularly of the way you may have internalised stereotypes which affect the way you view and, consequently, have particular expectations of children and families. Such internalised layers operate on both a conscious and subconscious level. Acknowledging the extent to which our personal belief and value system influences what we bring to the Early Years environment is an important 'first step' en route to anti-discriminatory practice.

Consider some of the 'building blocks of your own identity' (Dickins, 2002) – such as gender, ethnicity, class, religion and education.

- *Describe yourself in a sentence using these five attributes.*

- *Reflect on the significance of these in shaping who you are, what you believe and how you perceive others.*

- *In the EYP role as leader of practice, how do you ensure colleagues are aware of these influences on them and their roles?*

- *How, as a leader, do you give staff the skills and confidence to challenge appropriately overt inequality/ discriminatory practice they may witness?*

The Alliance for Inclusive Education (1990) offers nine core principles as indicative of commitment to inclusive practice. Use these as a further tool for reflection as you clarify your own personal values and beliefs:

- a person's worth is independent of their abilities or achievements;

- every human being is able to feel and think;

- every human being has a right to communicate and be heard;

- all human beings need each other;

- real education can only happen in the context of real relationships;

- all people need support and friendship from people of their own age;

- progress for all learners is achieved by building on things people can do rather than what they can't;

- diversity brings strength to all living systems;

- collaboration is more important than competition.

Before we move on to think about particular strategies that support inclusive practice, it is important to conclude this section by focusing on the values that children themselves are developing. Again, this is a complex matter and expansive discussion is beyond the scope of this publication but it is important to reflect here on S28 and think about how the values and attitudes demonstrated by the EYP can directly affect and influence children's own values. The EYFS framework reminds us that:

> *The attitudes of young children towards diversity are affected by the behaviour of adults around them and by whether all children and families using the setting are valued and welcomed.*

> (DCSF, 2008c: 1)

Rodd (2006) reminds us that many of the subjective and enduring attitudes we use to interpret messages we receive from others are formed by the age of five. From our understanding of child development, we know that young children from around the age of two are visually curious about the people and places around them. They take note of physical characteristics: height, weight, skin colour, hair style, clothing, etc.; of gender; and of some characteristics of disability – hearing aids, glasses, walking sticks, etc. But we do know that while such very young children speak without any socially constructed inhibitions, any questions or comments they make at this stage are **not** value-laden but merely an extension of their natural curiosity as they construct knowledge and understanding of their world. From the age of three years, some of their comments may appear to be value laden but these are almost always 'recycled adult comments' (Lindon, 2006: 47). Devising and implementing appropriate ways to challenge such comments when necessary is an important aspect of the EYP role. However, it is important to register your valuable role in modelling to children the application of fair approaches and how you treat everyone with equal concern; this includes children, staff, parents, other professionals and any visitors.

REFLECTIVE TASK

Young children's antennae readily tune in to both overt and subtle messages about who is 'better' than who and who is valued in society . . . and all this at a time when they are beginning to put together a picture of their own identity.

(Dickins, 2002: 17)

What are the implications of this for the EYP in modelling and leading equality practice? How do you support your colleagues to recognise, monitor and challenge, if inappropriate, subtle messages are being conveyed within the setting?

The key person

The appointment of the 'key person' and the organisation of this is addressed more fully in Chapter 5 but we note here how integral to good equality practice the key person role is in 'meeting the needs of each child . . . and responding sensitively to their feelings, ideas and behaviour, talking to parents to make sure that the child is being cared for appropriately for each family' (DCSF, 2008a: 37). The key person role is enshrined in the statutory requirements of the EYFS (DCSF, 2008a) and you will need to make sure that you understand the underpinning principles for the role and seek to empower and equip all staff in your setting for their roles as key persons. In larger settings, especially where staff work different shifts, it is best practice to designate a 'significant other' for each child to support the primary key person.

While the crucial roles of key person and significant other cannot be overemphasised, it is important to create appropriate means for sharing vital information with all relevant staff about each child – especially linked to their individual learning journeys and stories (Carr, 2001) and how these connect into wider organisational matters such as planning and monitoring the programme and partnership with families.

In a busy base room for 18 two- to three-year-olds, Liam is the key person for two-year-old Shafiq. But, as Shafiq attends the day nursery full-time from 8am until 6pm, Chloe has been appointed as co-key person for Shafiq. In this way, the nursery ensures that for most of the time that Shafiq is in nursery, either Liam or Chloe – or both of them – are also present and take lead responsibility for his well-being. Shafiq has been diagnosed with a hearing impairment (HI) and so once a week, a teacher from the local authority HI Education Service visits to work with Shafiq and to discuss his progress with one/both key workers and Shafiq's parents. Amina, the room leader, is an EYP and has overall responsibility for the programme and provision in the room.

What are the challenges to the EYP in ensuring that all relevant personnel are involved, can contribute to the weekly meetings and work in partnership together? What opportunities does this present for the EYP to demonstrate equality practice?

The significance of the early years of a child's life in shaping personal identity has long been identified. Particularly crucial factors in developing a sense of self come from the following: knowing our own name – and how people use and react to it; an understanding of what it means to be a 'boy' or a 'girl'; our place within our immediate family – parents, siblings and other close relatives; how we look and how people react to our looks; what we can do and cannot do – and the extent to which this matters to people; a growing sense of 'what we do in our family/community'; experiences of cultural traditions, mother/father roles, religious faith and other significant beliefs/values within their daily life (based on Lindon, 2006).

It is important to take a holistic view of identity and the individual child and understand that the formation of identity is a complex and dynamic process which, though central to childhood, may be modified throughout adult life (Dickins, 2002).

A young child experiences the important people in her/his life as:

> *'helping me manage through the day, thinking about me, knowing me well, sometimes worrying about me, getting to know each other so they can all do the "best" for me and talking together about me and to me.'*

- *How have you developed key person practice to ensure it reflects your ethos/policy for equality and/or inclusion?*

- *How do you support children, families and practitioners when unfamiliar cultural or linguistic differences are part of the experiences the child brings to the setting?*

- *What are the challenges you have faced/may face and how might you plan to meet these in future?*

Staff development opportunities

EYP S38 reminds you of the importance of identifying and accessing relevant professional development for yourself and of supporting others in their continuing professional development (we discuss this further in the final chapter of the book). There are many workshops and training programmes available both within local authority provision and nationally. The CD-ROM provided as part of the resource to support implementation of the EYFS framework (DCSF, 2008c) signposts a range of these to support EYFS practice in meeting the needs of the unique child and promoting equality practice. Do make sure you access this superb resource to the full.

Current inequalities

Despite the priority and financial investment given to Early Years provision in the past few years, there remain undoubted inequalities (Hirsch, 2007) and these should be a concern to all EYPs. A 2007 Report from the United Nations Children's Fund (UNICEF) makes for sobering reading, with the UK achieving only a very low ranking in a study of 21 comparably industrialised countries rating children's well-being by the time they reach the age of 15. Early reviews of Sure Start provision (such as Sure Start Keighley, 2005) suggested that families from minority ethnic groups were not always accessing the Early Years provision and services to which they were entitled. In 2010, the National Children's Bureau (NCB) launched a campaign 'Firm Foundations' (NCB, 2010) aiming to combat the effects of inequality and disadvantage. The Government recognises this is a key issue and has commissioned a six-year study, the Evaluation of Children's Centres in England (ECCE) (Department for Education (DfE)/NatCen, 2009–15) which particularly aims to assess the impact of children's centre provision in reducing inequalities in outcomes between the most disadvantaged children and the rest.

Edgington (2004) offers a useful checklist for awareness-raising in matters relating to equality practice. She asks you to consider how you have made yourself and your staff aware of the following: inequalities in society, inequalities in education, attitudes (including your own) which may lead to discrimination against some children and families, discriminatory language used or unthinking remarks made by staff, children, parents, visitors and practices within your own setting which may reinforce existing inequalities – especially admissions, transitions, communication with parents, and access to wider services (adapted from Edgington, 2004: 86).

CASE STUDY

Val *works as an EYP in a consultancy capacity across a small chain of private nurseries. The majority of these cater for the needs of white British children and families and the nursery environments and programmes reflect this. However, the neighbourhood of two of them is much more multicultural.*

How might Val lead practice to be more inclusive? In particular, what professional development opportunities might Val access for herself and/or develop for the nursery staff team?

CASE STUDY

Juan and Penny *co-lead a local pre-school in the local village hall. Historically, the setting has not catered for children with additional needs as such families had not registered for places. However, recently two families have requested places for their children: one has a significant medical condition and the other has mobility challenges.*

How might Juan and Penny best prepare themselves as leaders of practice to create an inclusive setting for such children? What action will they need to take in leading the staff to feel ready and skilled to manage inclusion on a daily basis?

How do we take best equality practice forward?

Discrimination – whether direct, indirect, intentional or unintentional – comes in many forms and sound reflective practice will include vigilance to any/all of these. Standard 18 offers a reminder that it is the task of the EYP to support and lead the creation of an inclusive community and S39 focuses on the role of the EYP in 'taking a constructively creative and critical approach towards innovation' (CWDC, 2010a: 89). The setting stories and reflective tasks that follow offer you an opportunity to consider innovative ways of moving equality practice forward in your own setting and in so doing demonstrate more effective anti-discriminatory practice. Guidance from the EYFS framework and other key documents (signposted at the end of the chapter) offer helpful pointers for practitioners in meeting children's diverse needs and helping all children to make the best possible progress. In particular, practitioners should:

- Extend the scope of individualised learning by providing challenging expectations and relevant, developmentally appropriate learning opportunities for babies and young children.

- Provide a safe and supportive learning environment, free from harassment, in which the contribution of all children and their families is valued and where racial, religious, disability and gender stereotypes and all expressions of discrimination or prejudice are challenged.

- Value the fact that families are all different – that children may live with one or both parents, with other relatives or carers, with same sex parents or in an extended family.

- Work with parents to identify learning needs and respond quickly to any area of particular difficulty.

- Plan appropriate opportunities that build on and extend all children's knowledge, experiences, interests and skills and develop their self-esteem and confidence in their ability to learn.

- Use a wide range of teaching strategies, based on children's learning needs.

- Provide a wide range of opportunities to motivate, support and develop children and help them to be involved, concentrate and learn effectively.

- Plan for each child's individual care and learning requirements, including the additional or different provision required to meet particular individual needs.

- Audit how accessible the setting is for children who use wheelchairs or other mobility aids or who are learning English as an additional language and take action to include a wider range of children.

- Work together with professionals from other agencies to provide the best learning opportunities for each individual child.

(DCSF, 2008c: 2–3)

REFLECTIVE TASK

Be realistic in your appraisal of how far the reality of your own practice and setting is from these 'ideals'. Where might you start in the development of more effective and innovative practice in your setting?

You are now encouraged to use this series of setting stories. These are not exhaustive but are intended to be a reflective tool as you consider the potential breadth of equality practice and focus on its application to your own role and setting, especially as you think about gathering evidence for S2, 4, 12, 18, 23 and reflect on the ways you challenge discrimination. Some of the case studies here may well describe experiences you have not encountered so far in your role but it is important that you engage with these, particularly reflecting on the value stance and attitudes of staff, children and families portrayed in them, as well as on possible action.

Best practice in respect for girls and boys

Scenario 1: Cassie is an EYP and works as a registered childminder. She is currently minding three children: a baby girl, Sophie, of nine months and two toddlers: Sophie's brother Damien, aged 26 months and Adela (different family), aged 27 months. Cassie is a committed, conscientious and reflective practitioner who is developing a more personalised approach to her practice by observing and building on the children's interests. Adela and Damien enjoy dressing up and both love the character 'Bob the Builder' from the popular TV series. Cassie has provided hard hats, fluorescent sleeveless jackets and other artefacts to support the children in their fantasy play which takes place mainly in the garden. However, Adela's mum, Mandy, talks to Cassie about Adela dressing up in 'boys' clothes' and the rough-and-tumble nature of her play. Mandy asks that Adela wears only 'girls' clothes' when she dresses up.

Cassie listens attentively to Mandy's concerns – aware, nonetheless, of her own personal strong disagreement with Mandy's stance. Cassie responds with an expression of positive regard for Mandy and encourages her to express the core of her concern. Adela is the youngest of four children, with three older brothers, and Mandy is very keen that Adela should be 'feminine' in every way. Over some weeks, Cassie works with Adela and Mandy to reassure Mandy that gender roles are not fixed or determined by role or fantasy play and that any attempts to stop Adela playing in her own way with her friend, Damien, would be virtually impossible and not helpful to her development. Cassie also introduced a wider range of dressing up clothes and fantasy play over time. For instance, she helped the children create a 'cave' using her dining room table covered in dark cloth, which could be lifted to make an entrance. She provided torches and boxes so they could develop the play.

REFLECTIVE TASK

> Boys' under-achievement in education has now become a global concern . . .The
> Early Years represent a significant opportunity for this to be addressed.
> *(Connolly, 2004: foreword)*

In what ways do you ensure that the needs of girls and boys are identified and met in your setting? How do you help lead everyone involved with the setting to understand an ethos that avoids stereotypes and challenges discrimination?

Best practice in respect of personal care

Scenario 2: 'Over the Rainbow' is a popular pre-school situated in a lively urban suburb and the majority of families using the setting are comfortably middle-class, with high economic stability. Four-year-old Jado, an only child, lives with his mum Caitlin, in the area and has attended the setting for about two months but has not settled very well. Jado's mum recently separated from his dad and Jado has been even more clingy and reluctant to come to pre-school since dad moved out of the family home. Jado is still not toilet-trained and shows no control over bladder or bowels and Caitlin is anxious not to put him under any additional pressure at this time. There is no diagnosis of a medical condition and Caitlin believes that Jado is just 'not ready' for toilet-training yet.

Sade, preparing for EYPS, is Jado's key person and seeks to be a reassuring and stable presence for Jado in the setting. She always takes time to talk to Caitlin, to find out what activities Jado enjoys at home (books and baking) and has encouraged her to stay with Jado in the sessions for the time being, although she notes that when his mum is there, Jado is very reluctant to do anything or play with any resources independently or with other children. It is clear that, while Caitlin wants to avoid any further stress for Jado, she is also rather embarrassed that he is the only four-year-old in the pre-school who is still wearing nappies. Some of the other boys in the group make overt comments about Jado and his nappies and Sade responds to these promptly and firmly but without judging the other boys, often diverting their attention to another topic. Jado is beginning to trust Sade and she is skilfully building on this by introducing books that the three of them can share together, and organising a baking activity with just one other child. One of the books, Sade has used is: *Pirate Pete's Potty Book* by Andrea Pinnington (2009). In discussion with Caitlin, Sade is also sharing the nappy-changing time and is using this time to make eye contact with Jado and talk to him about the pre-school.

REFLECTIVE TASK

What strategies would you implement to ensure your setting's practice was inclusive and met the specific needs of the following children?

- *a girl with sensitive or troublesome skin;*
- *a child with Afro-braided and beaded hair where the other children keep touching and playing with the beads;*
- *those who have their hair covered or wear particular types of clothes – such as children from Sikh or Exclusive Brethren families.*

Best practice for different kinds of families

Scenario 3: Sunny Days Nursery offers provision for over 50 children aged from three months to five years. In the pre-school room, for three- to five-year-olds, there is a team of four staff working with 18 children, led by Gill who is on the long pathway to EYPS. Gill is strongly committed to reflective practice and seeks to lead by example in all areas of practice and provision in the toddler room.

Recently a family has moved into the neighbourhood and their four-year-old boy, Rory, has joined the group. When Gill (who is Rory's key person) – along with the nursery manager – carries out the home visit prior to Rory starting at the nursery, she learns that his mum, Sheena, lives with a female partner, Bernadette. This information is shared naturally as Gill builds up a log about Rory ('All About Me') and asks about all the 'important others' in Rory's life. Gill clarifies what names Rory uses for Sheena ('Mum') and Bernadette ('Bernie') and whether he has any contact with his biological father (he doesn't).

This is the first time that some of the staff in the room have experienced a child with same-sex parents and one of them, Rosie, makes hostile and insulting comments to Gill about such families. Gill uses the opportunity to raise Rosie's awareness of her own personal value stance (to which she is entitled, although the hope is that she can learn to be less discriminating), but reminds her that such attitudes are easily transmitted to children and may affect the way Rosie relates to Rory. Gill makes sure that new books in the nursery reflect a range of different types of families: traveller families; families with children with additional needs; families where mum goes to work and dad stays at home, as well as families with same-sex parents, those with two mums/dads, parents who live separately, etc.

43

REFLECTIVE TASK

Reflect on how Gill tackled this situation. Would you have done anything differently in your setting? Does your setting cater for the needs of the diverse range of family structures that you might encounter?

Best practice for religious beliefs

Scenario 4: Sameena will shortly be returning to work as an accountant after the birth of her daughter, Sufia, who is 14 months old, and has registered her at Hey Diddle Diddle private nursery, near to her place of work. Tim is one of the staff in the under-twos room and he is assigned to be Sufia's key person. Tim, with the nursery manager, Kath – an EYP – goes to visit Sameena and Sufia prior to Sufia starting at Hey Diddle Diddle. Sameena and her family, as Muslims, have strong views that only women should take responsibility for a baby's care needs and Sameena shares this politely during the home visit.

Kath and Tim respond sensitively but explain the way the key person system is organised in the nursery and that all practitioners share the same role. They both express respect for the religious beliefs of Sameena and her family but take a clear stance that if the issue of female care is not negotiable for Sameena, then Hey Diddle Diddle is not able to meet the family's needs. Kath goes on to outline the alternative of childminding provision as a way that Sameena can guarantee that Sufia has exclusively female care.

REFLECTIVE TASK

This is a difficult area as there are many strongly held views affecting childcare practice by the different religious groupings in contemporary society. How well informed do you consider yourself to be about these? How might you have dealt with the situation above? In what way was Kath demonstrating skills as a leader of practice here?

Best practice in respect of food and mealtimes

Scenario 5: Staff in an urban children's centre are generally well prepared when it comes to accommodating a range of dietary needs which allow for the different cultural and religious groups in the area and also for those children with medical needs. Three new children, Meg, Jack and Adem, from traveller families, are placed in the 'Tigers' room for three- and four-year-olds, with liaison/support from the local authority Traveller Education Service (TRES). The children have not been away from their families before. In consultation with TRES and the children's families, Meg, Jack and Adem are each assigned a separate key person in order to best monitor their needs at this key time of transition.

While the children are slow to relate socially to the other children, they do gravitate towards each other during play and early observations are that they are using play purposefully and developmentally appropriately. It is the practice in the setting to use lunchtimes as social occasions with each key person sitting with his/her own key group. By week three, Meg, Jack and Adem are still showing signs of restlessness and anxiety at lunchtime and staff notice that they are eating very little.

The relevant staff members meet with the TRES liaison worker, EYP Ben, the children's centre teacher, together with the children's parents to work out how best to address this situation. It is agreed that, for the time being, Meg, Jack and Adem will sit together with Ben at a small table for their lunch. Ben decides to use a 'social story' approach with the children at lunch, allowing them to serve themselves from the various foods on offer. Once the children are more confident in eating, a staged approach to their inclusion in the usual lunchtime arrangements will then be negotiated.

REFLECTIVE TASK

What terminology/language do you use when applying equity practice to food and meal times? Would you use phrases like 'restricted' or 'limited' diet? What do such phrases imply? Your own value stance is important here, especially in the way you lead practice. How do you cater for the needs of children with allergies or medical conditions affecting their diet? Is there any difference to your practice if/when dietary needs are determined by religious beliefs?

Best practice in respect of disability and ill health

Scenario 6: Guy and Estelle's third baby, Jonni, now aged ten months, is born with a medical condition that requires him to be fed by tube and have regular physiotherapy to ease congestion on his lungs. Their two older children were minded by Carol, a registered childminder who is preparing for EYPS, before they went to school and Estelle wishes to return to work part-time though is anxious about the additional needs that Jonni has. Carol and Estelle meet two months before Estelle is due to start back at work and days/hours are negotiated when Jonni will be Carol's sole charge. For the month before Estelle starts at work, she and Carol spend half a day a week together to jointly mind Jonni so that Estelle can supervise Carol in feeding procedures. The local Portage worker joins them for one of these sessions too, and the three of them agree on a shared approach to Jonni's individual development plan.

REFLECTIVE TASK

What experience have you had in leading the policy and practice of your setting in meeting the additional needs of children related to a medical condition, or who have a Statement of SEN? Consider how you have supported colleagues to work in partnership with other agencies and the challenges and developments this has created.

Best practice for more able children

Scenario 7: In Tree Tops Pre-School, Archie, aged three-and-a-half, is able to read fairly fluently, recognises numbers to 100 and can do simple mental calculations involving addition and subtraction. His parents are anxious not to 'hothouse' Archie, whose progress is otherwise typical of his age. The group leader, Sam, on EYP, is Archie's key person but seeks to develop a whole team approach to the inclusion of Archie within the group. One of the team, Sandra, has a tendency to want to provide more formal opportunities (what Sandra believes to be 'school-type') in which Archie reads and performs mathematical operations and she brings in 'workbooks' that her own (older) children have used. She is observed 'testing' Archie by asking him to read to her and answer mental maths questions. Sandra refers to him as 'Little Einstein'.

Sam arranges a one-to-one meeting with Sandra to discuss the situation. She aims to get Sandra to understand the impact of her approach not only on Archie but on the other children. Her reaction is accentuating 'difference' between him and the rest in an unhelpful way. Of particular concern is the unconscious value stance that Sandra is demonstrating: that play is not the best medium for Archie's learning. Sam strongly believes that it is and that Archie needs to learn socially and collaboratively with others, while being offered appropriate developmental challenges through play-based activities suitable to his learning ability. This is not an easy time for Sam and Sandra's professional relationship but slowly they are able to work together more constructively for Archie's sake.

> ### REFLECTIVE TASK
>
> *What experience have you had to date of supporting young children of exceptional ability? Sometimes these children have additional needs, such as some diagnosed on the autistic spectrum. In what ways has Sam exercised effective leadership of practice here? How does this link to S1?*

Best practice in respect of different forms of communication

Scenario 8: Jean-Paul is two-and-a-half and has been in the UK for six months. His parents, Emilie and Raoul, came into the country as asylum seekers from a French-speaking country in Africa and the family now has refugee status. Emilie and Raoul are learning English but at home they speak mainly French to Jean-Paul who is not using much spoken language at all at the moment. Emilie has joined a local parent and toddler group so that she and Jean-Paul can develop friendships with other local families. Shazia, the coordinator of the parent and toddler group, is herself bilingual, with English as her second language, but does not speak French. One of the other parents, Kenny, is fairly fluent in French.

Emilie is committed to Jean-Paul being bilingual and Shazia, preparing for EYPS, understands the importance of this for the family. Together, Shazia, Emilie and Kenny work on a strategy which includes some use of French but mainly using English in the setting, and soon Jean-Paul is happy to leave Emilie's side and explore the range of play activities on offer with the other children.

REFLECTIVE TASK

Look at this guidance from the EYFS framework.

> *Practitioners should value linguistic diversity . . . provide opportunities for children to use their home language in play and learning . . . actively promote bi-lingualism as a strength . . . and encourage all children to learn some of the languages they hear around them . . . They should model this themselves by . . . greeting children and families in their home language.*
>
> *(DCSF, 2008c: 4)*

This guidance clearly reminds Early Years practitioners of the importance of a child's home language. How do you yourself model effective practice in building on the child's experience of language at home? How is this balanced with planning appropriate opportunities for all children to develop English? What are the challenges for the leader of practice here?

C H A P T E R   S U M M A R Y

This may have been a challenging chapter but you should see that the principles outlined in it provide sure and firm foundations for the leadership of equality practice which is fundamental to the EYP role. In the process of reviewing some of the key issues relating to equality and inclusive policy and practice, and the weight of law behind these, you have also been encouraged to grow in self-awareness about your own personal beliefs and value stance and to reflect on how these influence and impact on the children, families and staff in your setting as part of your leadership role. Throughout the case studies and reflective tasks there has been an implicit motif: that of challenging discriminatory practice in all its forms by modelling a positive approach to diversity.

Moving on

Having defined the new concept of leadership of practice, explored the existing literature and research studies on leadership in the Early Years and established the core element of equality practice for the role of EYP, we now turn to consider some of the essential qualities, skills and competencies required for the role. In some ways, this will build on the understanding of classic trait theories but we will argue that any of these qualities can be developed and nurtured both through training and practice.

Self-assessment questions

Siraj-Blatchford and Clarke (2000) offer a very useful framework for self-assessment which you will find helpful in your appraisal of your own equality practice as you prepare your evidence for EYP validation. This can be found at: http://www.multiverse.ac.uk/ViewArticle2.aspx?contentId=13590

1. In what ways has the position of our wider society in relation to diversity changed over the past 50 years or so? What has been the impact of this change on Early Years practice? (Answer: pages 32–33)

2. Why is the language and terminology relating to diversity so important? (Answer: page 33)

3. What do we need to think about when writing or reviewing policy statements? (Answer: page 35)

4. What do we know about the development of young children's attitudes to diversity (Answer: pages 37–38)

5. Why is the relationship between key person and individual child so crucial in equality practice? (Answer: pages 38–39)

6. What conclusions are being drawn about current inequalities in Early Years service provision from recent Sure Start evaluations and from the Pre-School Learning Alliance? (Answer: pages 40–44)

7. Highlight three of the key messages about equality practice that are emerging from the EYFS framework. (Answer: pages 41–42)

FURTHER READING

There are a number of helpful publications to support you in leading equality practice. Although published by the Government of 1997–2010, the following list remains available from the National Strategies website, http://nationalstrategies.standards.dcsf.gov.uk/search/earlyyears. They are particularly recommended and are available for download:

Confident, Capable and Creative: Supporting boys' achievements: Guidance for practitioners in the Early Years Foundation Stage (DCSF, 2007).

Supporting Children Learning English as an Additional Language (DCSF, 2007).

Identifying Gifted and Talented Learners: Getting started (DCSF, 2008).

Social and Emotional Aspects of Learning (SEAL): Improving behaviour, improving learning (DCSF, 2008).

Inclusion Development Programme – Supporting children with speech, language and communication needs: Guidance for practitioners in the Early Years Foundation Stage (DCSF, 2008).

Building Futures: Developing Trust – A focus on provision for children from Gypsy, Roma and Traveller backgrounds in the Early Years Foundation Stage (DCSF, 2009).

Building Futures: Believing in children – A focus on provision for Black children in the Early Years Foundation Stage (DCSF, 2009).

Inclusion Development Programme – Supporting children on the autistic spectrum (DCSF, 2009).

4 Leadership of reflective practice

CHAPTER OBJECTIVES

In this chapter, we explore in more detail the essential competences and traits required for the role of leader of practice. As our focus, we take the three generic skills required for the EYP role as identified by CWDC (2010a): decision-making based on sound judgement; attributes of leadership; and communication skills. The dimension of the EYP as a reflective practitioner and in leading others to become more reflective in their approach to practice is explored in depth. You will have an opportunity to use case studies and reflective exercises to support your thinking and to complete an audit of your own strengths and areas for development in these aspects of the role.

After reading this chapter you should be able to:
- reflect on the skills, qualities and attributes required for the role of leader of practice – in partcular, skills as a reflective practitioner;
- appraise critically your own strengths and areas for development in this area;
- apply your understanding to the preparation of your evidence for EYP validation.

This chapter is wide-ranging and will help you in your preparation of evidence against many of the Standards but focuses particularly on Standards 17, 18, 22, 24, 25, 28, 30, 33, 38 and 39.

Introduction

We have already identified the challenge of clearly defining the role of the EYP but in Chapter 1, the following were offered as some of the key attributes and skills for the role, with the EYP able to demonstrate:

- reflective and reflexive practice in her/his own role and skills in decision-making;

- sound knowledge and understanding of Early Years pedagogy: the holistic needs of all children from birth to five and competence in planning, implementing and monitoring within the Early Years Foundation Stage framework (DCSF, 2008a);

- strong values of the intrinsic worth of each child and all those in her/his world;

- the ability to role-model, lead and support others in high-quality practice;

- the ability to define a vision for practice within a setting;

- competence as an agent of change.

All Early Years practitioners should demonstrate certain core characteristics: a passion for and strong commitment to quality provision for young children; a flexible approach to practice; the capacity to work independently and as part of a team; skills in caring for, nurturing and teaching young children; patience; sensitivity; and a sense of humour. But in this chapter, we focus specifically on the attributes, skills and competences of the leader of practice. Your role in pedagogical leadership, particularly in leading delivery of the EYFS (DCSF, 2008a) is explored more fully in the next chapter. Here, some of the key attributes of leadership are addressed and, in particular, we consider how the EYP demonstrates skills as a reflective and reflexive practitioner and encourages these skills in others. Indeed, the focus on 'Reflective Tasks' throughout this book is, itself, indicative of how central to the role is this attribute.

The reflective practitioner: key to decision-making based on sound judgement

You may like to look back to Chapter 1 and the work of Boddy et al. (2005) on the role of the social pedagogue. We have identified that we can draw helpful parallels between the characteristics and attributes of the European model of the pedagogue and those required for the role of the EYP. The pedagogue should have high expectations of her/himself and others, including the children and staff in the setting. One of the key characteristics of the social pedagogue, highlighted by Boddy et al. (2005), is the ability to reflect critically on her/his own practice and on practice within the setting, with strong self-awareness. Whalley (2005a) refers to this as a key aspect of pedagogical leadership.

For you, then, skilled reflection as part of decision-making based on sound judgement is of crucial importance in preparing evidence to meet the EYP Standards. Indeed, the final two Standards (S38 and S39) focus specifically on these aspects and the strongest evidence is that which identifies your skills in the context of your role in leading practice. How do you show yourself to be a competent reflective practitioner and how do you then enable others to become more reflective in their practice? In particular, how do you demonstrate that you are able to analyse both strengths and areas for development within a setting or particular aspect of practice?

CASE STUDY

Maura, in Task 1 of the written tasks submitted during her final assessment for EYP status, describes and discusses her role in introducing treasure baskets to the baby room in her setting. This was a new aspect of practice to most of the staff team so Maura organised staff training and worked with the team on creating treasure baskets and establishing an appropriate supply of resources to develop these, working with parents and carers to gather these and keep staff informed of the babies' preferences and interests. She modelled the staff role in supporting and observing the babies with the baskets and provided the team with ongoing guidance and practical help. Maura also facilitated a session for corporate reflection and evaluation of the innovation with the staff team around two months after the treasure baskets were introduced. Note how Maura concludes her written report here:

1.6: Your personal learning	Standard
At the beginning of this project when I first introduced the idea and showed the Elinor Goldschmied video to the staff, I was aware that while most of them were very enthusiastic about the idea, one member of staff had real concerns about the safety of the babies. She was worried that using so many natural materials and 'from home' resources might be unhygienic and the resources not carry the appropriate safety mark. When I first heard this, I was very dismissive of her attitude and expressed my frustration. Almost immediately, however, I regretted this and realised that my approach was totally inappropriate and quite unprofessional. I apologised to the staff member concerned and invited her to share her concerns in more detail. It turned out that she hadn't understood the role of the adult in heuristic play nor had she heard what I'd said about the importance of keeping resources clean, checking and changing them regularly. In the end, she became one of the most enthusiastic team members and really applied herself to creating a basket for one of her key babies. She wrote some beautiful observations of the baby exploring an egg whisk. Through this, I realised the importance not only of checking that everyone has understood but of taking any concerns seriously and always trying to see the other's view point. In future, I would spend more time before introducing a new idea or aspect of practice trying to analyse and predict some of the negatives as well as the positives.	38 39

REFLECTIVE TASK

How is Maura demonstrating her skills as a reflective and self-aware leader of practice here?

Thinking critically

The concept of the reflective practitioner is now well established across the social sciences, thanks to the influence of key figures like John Dewey (1933), Donald Schön (1983) and others. Schön's work in particular has helped us realise that, as professionals, we are continually faced with new experiences and situations which we then frame in the light of previous experience; thus we are embedding reflection in practice. His work in distinguishing reflection *on* action from reflection *in* action is particularly helpful. Craft and Paige-Smith (2008: 89) describe this as the difference between 'thinking on your feet' (reflection in action) and 'thinking after the event' (reflection on action). It is, in fact, writers such as Craft and Paige-Smith (2008), Leeson (2007) and Trodd (2005) who offer specific and practical guidance. Trodd (2005: 3) describes the reflective Early Years practitioner as '. . . professional and competent . . . continuously seeking to improve (their) practice' and goes on to describe the key component of reflective practice as the capacity to 'think critically'. This includes taking personal responsibility for the way we work with children, families and colleagues, the capacity to work autonomously and to manage change thoughtfully. Reflective leaders show sensitivity to others, drawing on evidence to ensure the validity of their practice now and for the future. This provides a secure base for sound judgement.

Let's take Trodd's (2005) focus of the reflective practitioner as a 'critical thinker' and explore what we mean by this. 'Critical thinking' as a concept is not easy to define and some of the definitions themselves require a lot of thought! For instance, Paul and Elder (2006: xvii) define it as 'the art of thinking about thinking in order to make thinking better', which is an interesting notion but does not, in itself, give any clues about how to think critically. Fisher (2001) helpfully breaks critical thinking down into component skills:

- the ability to compare and contrast;

- understanding of bias;

- awareness of values and beliefs;

- the ability to interpret and clarify expressions and ideas;

- the ability to question the credibility of claims;

- the ability to analyse and evaluate from different perspectives and make decisions.

(Based on Fisher, 2001: 1–14)

EYP is a graduate-level status and so all EYPs who have studied up to this level should have developed and demonstrated critical thinking skills. However, not all EYPs graduate in Early Childhood Studies or related subjects so it is useful here to consider the application of these critical thinking skills to the EYP role. As you prepare for validation, the focus is on evidence of the skills in practice, rather than in academic written form. Use the reflective task below to focus on your own practice and how you believe you are demonstrating these skills:

Table 4.1 Critical thinking skills

Critical thinking skills	Example	Your own reflection on practice
The ability to compare and contrast	Sian has been allocated a budget through her LA to develop the outdoor provision in the pre-school she leads. She demonstrates skills in being able to appraise alternative layouts and resources she might use for this task.	
Understanding of bias	Mark is the co-leader of the pre-school room in a children's centre and a new child is starting whose family belongs to the Jehovah's Witnesses. As a child, Mark had neighbours who belonged to this religion group and he is aware that he must be careful not to allow this to lead to stereotypical thinking.	
Awareness of values and beliefs	Cynthia works with Mark as his co-leader. She herself is deeply religious and belongs to the Seventh Day Adventists. As a reflective and critical thinker, Cynthia is aware that her own beliefs could affect the way she views the new child and adopts a professional approach which shows unconditional positive regard for the child.	
The ability to interpret and clarify expressions and ideas	Marie is a childminder who has recently attended training on 'Sustained, shared learning with children'. In preparing to cascade this within her local Childminding Network, she makes sure she has synthesised the essential 'messages' from the training but also works hard to make the ideas meaningful and accessible to the others so they, too, capture her enthusiasm and want to apply them into their own practice.	
The ability to question the credibility of claims	Leroy, an EYP in an independent setting, had the opportunity to visit Early Years settings in Denmark. Many of these were based on forest school principles with most of the learning taking place outdoors. Based on his observations of the children's play and the staff roles, he was able to ask critical questions about the staff's understanding of pedagogy.	
The ability to analyse and evaluate from different perspectives and make decisions	Ayesha works alongside the children's centre teacher and has specific responsibility for the twice weekly 'Stay and Play' sessions for parents and under-twos. A local business has agreed to finance the development of a bespoke base for these sessions so they can be held daily. Ayesha consults with parents, staff, LA advisers and also observes the children's play so that decisions made about the development reflect all perspectives.	

Self-awareness

In the last chapter, we identified the importance of the EYP having a strong sense of self and a high degree of self-awareness in leading practice. Moyles (2006: 14) reminds us that self-identity cannot be taken as a given but has to be 'achieved and sustained by a process of reflection'.

Brookfield's approach to critical reflection includes the suggestion that we look at reality through 'four critical lenses: our own viewpoint; our colleagues' viewpoint; the viewpoint of the learners; and the viewpoint offered by theoretical literature' (Brookfield, 1995, cited in Trodd, 2005: 4). Arguably, these four perspectives will result in well-informed judgements.

Leeson (2007: 149) suggests that one of the most useful models for reflection in Early Years practice is that offered by Ghaye and Ghaye (1998) which highlights different levels of reflection:

- **descriptive** – giving an account of the incident;
- **perceptive** – making links between the description and one's own feelings;
- **receptive** – allowing ourselves to be open to different perspectives on the account;
- **interactive** – creating links between one's learning here and future action;
- **critical** – questioning accepted practice in a creative and constructive manner, developing new theories and ways of working for oneself and others.

Hallet (2004) breaks this down into simple question format, suggesting that essentially, the reflective practitioner needs to be self-questioning. As you apply the leadership skills required for the EYP role, you should also encourage other practitioners to ask of themselves:

- What kind of practitioner am I?
- What kind of practitioner do I want to be?
- How do the children view me?
- How do my colleagues view me?
- How do the parents view me?
- How do I want others to see me?

(Based on Hallet, 2004: 48)

By reflecting not only on policy and practice but on the way we carry out our roles and others' perceptions of us, we are able to analyse whether things are as they should be or whether changes are needed and to base these on sound judgement.

Think of a routine activity that is part of your current role – such as reading stories to children, supporting their care needs (feeding, changing, etc.), engaging with them in outdoor play, etc. Use the questions above to reflect on the type of practitioner you are and/or would like to be. How do you know how others perceive you?

Leading others as reflective practitioners

Reflective dialogue (Anning and Edwards, 2006) is a core component of this and includes constructive discussion with key others, especially colleagues. Thus, it becomes the 'vehicle for knowledge exchange and joint knowledge construction' (Anning and Edwards, 2006: 149) There are strong grounds to understand this as a key part of the role of the leader of practice, especially in decision-making. Indeed, this underpins EYP S33 where you should demonstrate that you can: 'establish and sustain a culture of collaborative and cooperative working between colleagues' (CWDC, 2010a: 76).

In part, this aspect of the EYP role can be seen as that of the mentor or critical friend to colleagues. These two roles are not exactly the same – though there are some overlaps. In order to develop a better understanding of the mentor or critical friend roles, it is helpful firstly to consider how you yourself have been mentored or who has acted as critical friend to you.

Mentoring in the early years is a dynamic system of advice and support in the context of ongoing professional training and development which makes sense of reflective practice.

(Callan, 2006: 10)

(A critical friend), is a person who asks provocative questions, provides data to be examined through another lens, and offers critiques of a person's work as a friend . . . taking time to understand the context of the work presented and the outcome that the person . . . is working towards.

(Costa and Kallick, 1993: 50)

As part of your preparation for EYP validation, you might identify someone to act as your mentor or critical friend, or you might have one allocated to you. Think, now, of your experience of being mentored in your work generally as a leader of practice. How important is this in helping you see practice from the perspective of a trusted colleague? How does this support your leadership role?

Your role as mentor to colleagues needs to be constructed and interpreted flexibly, evolving as effective support for an individual colleague or team within an environment which is rooted in professional learning and reflection. Further perspectives of the role are provided by Rodd (2006: 172) who proposes that mentoring of others by early childhood leaders should be viewed not as a 'supervisory' or hierarchical relationship but as a 'special ongoing personal relationship . . . based on the development of rapport, mutual trust, respect and openness to learning'. This suggests that, as a mentor to others, you need to establish a sensitive and responsive connection to those whom you are leading. What emerges from this understanding of the role is the potential for you, as a mentor, to mutually benefit from the mentoring relationship. This resonates with the concept of a 'community of learners' (Wenger, 1998) where each is engaged in a process of collective learning.

You might find it helpful to think about the specific skills and behaviours that are demonstrated in the process of supporting and mentoring others:

- demonstrate professional expertise and model effective practice;

- listen actively and provide open, constructive feedback;

- prioritise opportunities for professional dialogue and organise your time for managing mentoring conversations;

- communicate clearly and ensure there is mutual understanding;

- include open questions and clarify any misconceptions;

- acknowledge the significance of non-verbal communication within the mentoring process. Ensure your own non-verbal communication supports mentoring conversations;

- appreciate different learning styles and consider various approaches;

- promote reflection, positive thinking, enquiry and investigation;

- encourage practitioners to be innovative when seeking to find realistic solutions;

- identify opportunities for practitioners to gain experience and deepen their understanding of effective practice;

- suggest additional support that is available and accessible for the practitioner;

- promote the practitioners' confidence and self-esteem;

- offer practitioners encouragement to take on more responsibility and initiative for their own development.

(Adapted from CUREE, 2005)

As you reflect on the mentoring role, examine the following case study and carry out the Reflective Task suggested.

Ros, an EYP in a children's centre

Ros is mentoring Ellie, a practitioner running a weekly support group for parents and carers. Ellie had recognised that members of the group were interested in using some story boxes at home. While on a local authority course on 'Using Stories', Ellie had developed the boxes, which contained interactive, multi-sensory props to use alongside story sessions and she had demonstrated their use with the group. She thought that if the parents and carers made some story boxes in the group sessions for children to take home, this would help to develop closer links with the group and be beneficial for the children; however, she was unsure how to proceed. Ros encouraged Ellie to examine some options for developing a group project on producing story box resources and summarised the key points at the end of the discussion. Ros arranged to meet with Ellie in the following week to review these points, consider any further concerns and develop an action plan.

These were some of the questions Ros explored with Ellie during their discussion.

- *Do you plan to involve the children in the project and would their interests be taken into account when selecting stories?*

- *How might other practitioners be engaged in this work and how do you think this project could be related to the wider practice of the setting?*

- *Do we need to ensure that resources are safely returned and have you considered who might have responsibility for maintaining the resources?*

- *Have you thought about obtaining feedback on the project and, if so, how do you anticipate that feedback can be collected and used to inform future development?*

Using these questions in the conversation helped to acknowledge and tackle initial concerns about the project. Different options were then openly explored to locate strategies to facilitate its implementation. Future meetings and review of progress would involve practitioner reflection and stakeholder feedback to aid review of the project and highlight possible modifications that may be required.

Consider how Ros supported Ellie and facilitated the development of an action plan for the project. Refer to the groups of Standards for EYPS and note any particular Standards which you think are pertinent to this case study. Look out for links between Standards, 'the knowledge and understanding outlined in the first six Standards will inform all aspects of practice covered in the section "effective practice"' (CWDC, 2010a: 8).

Effectiveness as a mentor

Your developing role in leading others is itself core to reflective practice. Part of this will include evaluation of your role in mentoring others. Mentees themselves will provide useful indicators of your effectiveness and you might think about how you might get such feedback from them and how you could use this to analyse this aspect of your leadership role. Your own mentor/critical friend might also share reflections with you as you continue to explore your leadership skills.

Your ability to reflect on your mentoring role can be a powerful tool in helping you to identify areas of practice that you feel are more successful and those that require greater focus. Indicators of successful mentoring include:

- changes in behaviour and improvements to practice;
- increased satisfaction and motivation;
- decreased stress;
- changes in attitudes, empowerment to act and longer-term impact;
- impact or influence on others, in the setting and beyond;
- sustained quality improvement.

It is also useful to consider some limitations of mentoring, such as when mentors:

- have their own agendas;
- encourage practitioners to replicate themselves;
- promote dependency;
- maintain the status quo;
- lack time for effectively managing their role;
- ignore the challenge of an unsuitable 'match' with their mentee.

(Adapted from Bush and Middlewood, 2005: 167–68)

Integrating knowledge into practice

A key element of reflective practice lies in the practitioner's skill in applying theoretical knowledge to real experience. Indeed, Ghaye and Ghaye (1998: 3) refer to reflection as 'practice with principle'. As an EYP, you are required to demonstrate skills in integrating knowledge into practice, particularly in the way you make decisions. The first group of EYP Standards (S1–6) is entitled 'Knowledge and Understanding' and requires you to have a significant bank of theoretical knowledge: about children's development, about the EYFS framework, about the relevant legislation and regulation relating to Early Years provision and practice. These standards, however, require far more than just knowledge. It is your skills in reflecting on the application of this to your practice which are crucial; you can demonstrate these through personal reflection and reflective dialogue with others.

REFLECTIVE TASK

Think of two examples of how you have made strong connections between your understanding of relevant theory or something you have read and your practice. What decisions did you make? How do these examples exemplify your skills in reaching sound judgements and as a leader of practice?

The reflective practitioner: an effective communicator

One of the most critical elements in effective leadership is that of interpersonal skills. We will consider the quality required of an effective leader more comprehensively in Chapter 7 when we focus on the teamwork elements of leadership but here we focus on the personal: on the individual skills and attributes which are so important for leadership of practice. Indeed, it is vital that you are able to articulate your own reflections to colleagues and that you are able to communicate effectively with them so that you are able to support their reflective thinking. Effective communication, then, is about conveying your message to other people clearly and unambiguously and about receiving, without distortion, the information that others wish to convey to you. 'Communication', of course, transcends the 'verbal' and includes those non-verbal indicators, such as gesture, posture, facial expression, eye contact and tone of voice which are as important as the actual words used; arguably, they are more so in some interactions (see, for instance, research carried out by Mehrabian in 1981). You might like to think about how you communicate non-verbally and how others perceive the non-verbal indicators that you demonstrate.

As we have identified, leaders in early childhood are predominantly female. Indeed, it can be argued that the development of the Early Years profession has been shaped to a large extent by the position of women in society (Ebbeck and Waniganayake, 2003). Historically, this is reflected in the low pay and status of Early Years (mainly female) practitioners. This, in turn, can be seen to have some bearing on communication patterns in Early Years leadership. Traditionally, women have been 'reluctant' to demonstrate confidence in the leadership role and have not always asserted their skills as competent and effective communicators (Pound, 2008). Children's workforce development in the UK is, though, continuing to create a growing sense of empowerment among women leaders in Early Years. Rodd (2006: 31–34) offers a useful critique of leadership and gender, though there is the risk of over-simplification here. She argues that the traditional mode of leadership is considered to be more male in orientation with communication styles characterised by control, power, domination and competition. A study in the 1970s by Hennig and Jardim (cited in Rodd, 2006) suggests that the attributes of a feminine model of leadership would contrast greatly with these 'male' characteristics and would focus on communication styles that emphasise relationships, consensus, collaboration and flexibility.

Interestingly, research by Kinney in 1992 (cited in Rodd, 2006) suggests that in early childhood settings, there is no measurable difference in the actual functions of leadership carried out by men or women and the essential tasks remain the same regardless of the leader's gender. These are empowering, restructuring, taking responsibility for teaching and learning, acting as a role model and demonstrating effective communication skills through being open and questioning about all aspects of practice. However, Kinney's research did highlight the fact that the style of leadership demonstrated by men and women differs. Women generally use a facilitating style and men a more authoritarian approach (Whalley, 2002).

Although not directly relevant to current discussion, it is interesting to note that, paradoxically, while the glass ceiling remains a real barrier to aspiring women leaders in many professions, the great majority of EYPs to date are women. Indeed, it is worth noting here that many of the early pioneers of childcare practice and provision were strong, determined women – such as Maria Montessori (1870–1952) and Margaret McMillan (1860–1931) – and that the majority of leading contemporary writers on Early Years are women. We now face the significant challenge of encouraging more men to pursue careers in Early Years practice to counterbalance the perceived 'feminised' culture by which it is characterised. Leadership in the Early Years transcends gender and it is the style of communication and leadership which is critical, with a facilitating model being the one considered to be the most appropriate:

> The future of management is 'female' with the feminine attributes of cooperation, communication, diplomacy and insight preferred over the traditional male attributes of competition, aggression, hierarchy and logic.

> (Grant, cited in Rodd, 2006: 31)

Assertive leadership

As we have seen already in this chapter, part of the reflective process includes the capacity for greater understanding of oneself, one's own reactions and responses to people and situations. As an EYP, you will need a strong self-confidence, too, which will stem – in part, at least – from the value you place on your role and your belief about the overall place and contribution of effective Early Years practice to wider society. Furthermore, from such healthy self-confidence will come appropriate self-assertion: the skill to convey calmly, competently and confidently your own feelings (positive and negative), opinions, beliefs and needs in such a way that does not negatively affect the self-esteem of anyone else (Dryden and Constantinou, 2004). Of course, the reality is much more challenging than the rhetoric. But with healthy self-awareness will come understanding of situations or people to which/whom you behave, communicate and respond passively, aggressively or manipulatively rather than assertively. As a leader of practice, you have significant responsibility in role-modelling an assertive approach to your colleagues.

'Assertiveness' has been identified as a necessary skill for all practitioners if they are to be 'proactive, initiate necessary action and be able and prepared to put forward (their) own judgements' (CWDC, 2010c: 19). Although the context for this statement is primarily that of working with other professionals, it nonetheless picks up on an important dimension of the EYP role. Behaving and communicating assertively is, of course, far easier in theory than practice and none of us can realistically remain calm, competent and confident all the time! It is helpful to work out in which situations we find ourselves behaving and communicating passively or aggressively. Experience tells us that these are not the ways to develop healthy relationships. Being assertive does not remove the anxiety and stress which is part of our lives and relationships, but greater understanding of our own – and others' behaviour – can help. Mary Stacey puts it this way: 'A positive energetic presence will inspire others more than a tense and worried one' (Stacey, 2009: 43).

PRACTICAL TASK

Use the following scenarios to identify if the leader in question is responding/ communicating passively, aggressively, or manipulatively. In the right hand column, identify a more appropriately assertive response.

Table 4.2 Leadership responses

Scenario	Type of response	Alternative appropriate assertive response
Carla, a childminder, fails to make eye contact with a parent who is late collecting her baby for the third day running. Carla is non-communicative to the parent, merely handing over the child's bag.		
Pete works in a Sure Start local project and ignores a negative comment he overhears from a parent that men shouldn't work in Early Years settings.		
Claudette is lead practitioner of the baby room in a private nursery. She shouts at one of her members of staff who has failed to dispose of a child's nappy in an appropriate way.		
Morna is a lead practitioner in a children's centre. When one of the parents raises a significant concern about practice in the nursery, Morna uses self-disclosure to share some of her own pressing domestic issues.		
Kezia is supervisor of a pre-school. A student on placement spends a lot of time with one child, reading one book after another to him. Kezia storms into the book area, takes the book off the student and states: 'That's enough!'		

A consistently assertive communication style remains one to which most of us can only aspire but within the EYP role. It is important that you cultivate a self-assured approach in a variety of situations where you have opportunity to lead approach and try and avoid the pitfalls of either passivity or aggression.

C H A P T E R   S U M M A R Y

In this chapter, we have identified some of the essential traits, characteristics and qualities required by the EYP in the role of leader of practice. In particular, skills in reflective practice that are key to effective decision-making have been highlighted. While you have reflected on your own personal skills and attributes, as a competent and confident communicator, through the case studies offered and other exercises, you may well have begun a personal skills audit. At the end of the chapter you are encouraged to formalise this. This all connects very clearly to EYP S38 and S39 where your leadership role must be supported with skilled reflection and analysis both of the situation and your own reactions, responses and relationships. As a leader of practice, you recognise that you, too, are a learner and that your role requires a confident, respectful and assertive approach as you lead by example.

Moving on

In the next chapter, the focus moves from the particular skills and qualities required to lead practice effectively to the specific role of the EYP as a pedagogical leader. We explore current understandings of Early Years pedagogy and the role of the EYP in leading delivery of the Early Years Foundation Stage. This will provide opportunity for you to reflect on and refine your understanding of the pedagogical base for your own practice and the values you hold about your role as a pedagogue.

Self-assessment: personal skills audit

You now have the opportunity to formalise your reflections on this chapter and to identify both your own strengths and areas for development. You can then devise an action plan to show how you might address any areas for development. When planning action, think about the following:

- **Prioritising:** Which of the areas highlighted for development needs to be addressed immediately/in the medium term/long term?

- **Aims/intentions:** What exactly are you aiming for? It is important to spend time clarifying this at the outset.

- **Support:** The role of a critical friend and mentor is important here but equally who else in the setting do you need to support you as you address this area?

- **Resources:** Is there a training programme you might access? A course of further study or training you might join? Books or other resources for purchase? What about budget implications here?

Table 4.3 Personal skills audit

SELF AUDIT:

Skills/Attributes	Experience (in current or previous setting)	Personal strengths	Areas for development	Action points
• The application of critical thinking skills to decision-making				
• Self-questioning and personal responsibility/accountability				
• Willingness to engage with a professional critical friend				
• Skills in mentoring colleagues				
• Reflective dialogue with colleagues				
• Effective and sensitive communication, including awareness of non-verbal indicators				
• Assertiveness				

ACTION PLAN:

Action needed	Aims/intentions	Timescale	People involved	Resources/cost implications	Criteria for success	Date for review

- **Criteria for success**: How will you know you've achieved your aim?

- **Review**: Any action – personal or organisational – needs to be reviewed and a date should be set for this initial review at the outset.

Craft, A. and Paige-Smith, A. (2008) Reflective practice. In Miller, L. and Cable, C. (eds) *Professionalism in the Early Years*. Oxon: Hodder Education.

Leeson, C. (2007) In praise of reflective practice. In Willan, J., Parker-Rees, R. and Savage, J. *Early Childhood Studies* (2nd edn). Exeter: Learning Matters.

5 Pedagogical leadership

CHAPTER OBJECTIVES

Leading and supporting colleagues to effect change and improve outcomes for children are distinguishing attributes of the role of EYPs (CWDC, 2010a). This book acknowledges the variety of dimensions to the EYP's role in leading and supporting Early Years practice. In this chapter, we explore the position of the EYP as a pedagogical leader whose role is essentially concerned with effective delivery of the EYFS in order to promote positive outcomes for young children. The concept of Early Years pedagogy, which is premised on an understanding of how children learn and develop, is initially explored. We then consider the various aspects of the EYP's role in pedagogical leadership, which is supported by case studies.

After reading this chapter you should be able to:
- define your understanding of the significance and scope of the EYP's role as a pedagogical leader of practice;
- critically reflect on aspects of Early Years pedagogy, including your role as a pedagogical leader within the context of your setting;
- consider further areas of development for your pedagogical leadership.

This chapter makes reference to several EYP Standards, particularly those within the groups 'Knowledge and Understanding' (S1–S6), 'Effective Practice' (S7–S24) and 'Personal Professional Development' (S37–S39). It builds on the definition of 'Early Years pedagogy' and introduction to the role of the 'pedagogue' outlined in Chapter 1. You are encouraged to consider this subject alongside other areas of the EYP's role in providing leadership and support; in particular, reflective and reflexive practice considered in the last chapter, the skills and qualities that are required to undertake the role of leading changes to practice (Chapter 6), partnership working with colleagues and families (Chapter 7) and partnership working within multi-agency teams (Chapter 8).

Introduction

The EYP's role as a pedagogical leader of practice is concerned with developing overall provision that meets children's present needs and promotes their future learning and development (DCSF, 2009b). In leading effective practice within the EYFS, it is important that you demonstrate sound understanding of theoretical views of children's learning and development, and the factors which can influence this, and are able to communicate this information to colleagues. It is in defining the pedagogical base for your own practice that you will be supporting others to do likewise. A key part of this involves deep awareness of your own values and beliefs about Early Years provision and practice. The role of pedagogical leadership is complex and, in this chapter, we explore some of its challenges. You will have the opportunity to reflect on a range of strategies to help clarify your own thinking about the pedagogical base of your own practice and, through case study examples of EYPs' pedagogical leadership and relevant tasks, reflect on this important element of your leadership role.

Early Years pedagogy: the context

The term 'pedagogy' has a general meaning within the current policy framework of Early Years provision. It has been defined as:

> *the understanding of how children learn and develop, and the practices through which we can enhance that process. It is rooted in values and beliefs about what we want for children, and supported by knowledge, theory and experience.*
>
> (Stephen and Pugh, 2007, cited in DCSF, 2009a: 4)

When exploring Early Years pedagogy, consideration needs to be given to the highly influential factors that have shaped current perspectives and approaches to practice. These factors include theoretical views of childhood and children's development, the work of the pioneers of Early Years provision, findings from contemporary research studies of Early Years practice and global approaches to Early Years provision (Allen and Whalley, 2010). This chapter does not seek to provide a detailed exploration of these factors; rather, it considers how they influence the role of Early Years pedagogical leadership. Early Years pedagogy must also be contextualised within a wider shifting policy arena, which places the individual needs of the child and their family at the centre of a more holistic approach to the provision of children's services. This is discussed further in Chapter 8.

Approaches to Early Years pedagogy have been predominantly influenced by contemporary theoretical views about children's learning and development (Broadhead et al., 2010; Anning et al., 2009). As a graduate leader, you are expected to model an informed and reflective approach to practice, which will include a high level of knowledge and understanding of theoretical views of children's learning and development. This will help you to understand how changing views of children's development have emphasised the practitioner's role in providing suitable contexts to support children's learning in particular areas, which gives a heightened importance to the role of the pedagogical leader (Bowman et al., 2000).

REFLECTIVE TASK

How do you ensure you keep abreast of contemporary thinking about young children's learning and development? What priority do you give to this? How do you share your updated learning with colleagues?

In recent years, a move towards a clearer understanding of the various aspects of Early Years pedagogy has been provided by the EYFS statutory framework (DCSF, 2008a), which asserts a principled approach to practice premised on its four guiding themes: *A Unique Child, Positive Relationships, Enabling Environments and Learning and Development*. The interrelated EYFS themes and their linked commitments reflect the centricity of the individual child in current Early Years practice. They offer a common language for conceptualising and practising elements of Early Years pedagogy, which embraces child development, partnership working with parents, the significance of relationships, understanding areas of learning and establishing secure and challenging play-based indoor and outdoor environments (DCSF, 2009a).

The EYFS emphasises how children's learning is supported through practitioners' respectful and caring relationships and their skilful engagement with children. This role includes, for instance, supporting and inspiring children and encouraging their willingness and interest in continuing the process of making sense of the world (Samuelsson and Carlsson, 2008). Pedagogical leaders must support practitioners to reflect on their interactions with children and identify the impact of these on children's learning. This focus on high-quality interactions is considered 'as the strongest pedagogical tool that adults can bring to their work' (DCSF, 2010a: 12). We will return to consider the significance of practitioners' pedagogical approaches later in this chapter but we first explore the role of pedagogical leadership.

The EYP's role of pedagogical leadership

Primarily, an EYP's role of pedagogical leadership is concerned with effectively implementing the EYFS framework. Essential sources of guidance to help EYPs establish and develop effective pedagogical practices within their settings are found in the EYFS Practice Guidance (DCSF, 2008b), the Principles into Practice cards (DCSF, 2007) and the EYFS CD-ROM (DCSF, 2008d). Additionally, the EYP Standards support EYPs with the leadership of Early Years pedagogy and implementation of the EYFS (CWDC, 2010a). Standards within the group 'Effective Practice' (S7–S24) are of specific interest to your role in pedagogical leadership, as they provide outcome statements for the different aspects of EYPs' practice which promote all children's well-being, and support and extend their development (CWDC, 2010a). In realising the aims of the EYFS, pedagogical leaders should support practitioners in ensuring that:

- children experience effective provision in Early Years settings for their learning, care and development, which enables them to progress (S7–S13, S17–S24);

- they provide for equality of opportunity and anti-discriminatory practice so that every child is included and not disadvantaged (S5, S12, S18);

- they create the framework for partnership working between parents and professionals (S31);

- they improve quality and consistency by means of a universal set of standards (S1, S4, S5, S24);

- they lay a secure foundation for future learning through provision for children's learning and development that is planned around children's individual needs and interests and informed by continuous observational assessment (S8–S13).

(Adapted from DCSF, 2008a: 7)

In your role as a pedagogical leader, you will be required to establish, and help others to make effective personalised provision for the children within your settings (S13); for instance, by supporting practitioners to undertake observations and assessments of children (S10) and to review children's learning and development with them (S22) and with their parents (S32). The benefits of effective leadership of this approach have been recognised by Ofsted (2008) in their report on organisation, leadership and management in Early Years settings. Ofsted noted that, in the most effective settings, the key person has a strong knowledge of the child and seeks to ensure provision is focused on their holistic needs, which enables the child to build on what they already know and make good progress in their learning and development.

As a pedagogical leader, therefore, you are required to support practitioners to construct a broad image of the child by gathering information from different sources about, for example, their play choices, views and interests, their interactions with adults and other children and their responses to different situations and routines (DCSF, 2009b). You should also assist practitioners in analysing and using this information to support children's learning and development. This process is explored in the following practical task.

PRACTICAL TASK

The following task enables you to think about how practitioners gather and act on information about the child.

Complete the second column in the table below by reflecting on specific information you have gathered about a child or children in your setting, thinking about the various sources on which you can draw; for instance, parents and carers, colleagues, and other professional partners. In the third column, think about some examples from your practice to demonstrate how you have acted upon such information to support children's learning and development.

By completing the above task, you will have identified how the process of gathering and, crucially, interpreting and acting on information about children enables provision to be targeted more effectively at their individual needs. This, in turn, helps children to feel respected and valued as an individual. When leading practice in your setting you should aim, therefore, to encourage practitioners to identify and act on the information from collective sources in order to more effectively meet the needs of children in their setting. This action has particular relevance for S10–S14.

As you develop an understanding of your role of pedagogical leadership in your setting, it is important to consider how your values, knowledge and experience influence how you interpret and perform this role.

Table 5.1 Responding to information from a child

Aspects of a child's learning and development	Relevant information about a child or children in your setting	How you have acted on this information?
Play choices		
Interests and dislikes		
Views		
Interactions with other children and adults		
Response to different situations and routines		
Needs and feelings		
Present competences		
Current goals		
Preferential learning style		

(Source: adapted from DCSF, 2009b: 5)

Pedagogical leadership: values and beliefs

Early Years pedagogy is influenced by the views of the practitioner, policy-makers and also those of the wider society about broader perspectives of children, learning and the underlying rationale of provision (Stephen, 2010). Assumptions and values inform our practice and shape our views on what children do and say at different stages of their development and within different sociocultural contexts (Lancaster, 2010). The following case study illustrates how an EYP's development of outdoor play provision was under-pinned by a firm belief in the value of the outdoor environment.

CASE STUDY

Jenna, an EYP in a private nursery

'I have found that, when given the choice, the outdoors is where most children want to be. Parents also highly value outdoor experience; they are aware that nursery provision gives their child access to opportunities outdoors that they may not otherwise experience. This made it especially important for me to develop this practice within my setting.

In thinking about outdoor provision, the main idea that we must hold in our minds is that the outdoors is different to indoors in many ways. These differences are what make it special and important. Planning must be carried out as much as the indoor environment, regardless of the weather. The special nature of the outdoors fits the ways young children want to be; it gives a strong rationale and justification for developing rich outdoor provision and building in as much access to it as possible.

It is important that all practitioners have a clear understanding of their roles and responsibilities: this will include being clear, positive and confident about their roles in supporting good-quality play outdoors; planning and organisational systems that ensure every child receives an enjoyable and challenging learning and development experience, tailored to meet their individual needs.

A deeper understanding of safety, challenge and risk must be developed. It is vital that adults help children gain a healthy approach to physical, mental and emotional risk and to learn how to keep themselves safe: the outdoors has much to offer here. Risk management must be seen by practitioners as a highly useful tool for providing the safe framework that enables appropriately rich and challenging experiences for all children.'

REFLECTIVE TASK

Reflecting on this case study, consider:

- *Which aspects of outdoor provision does Jenna value and why?*

- *What challenges might Jenna encounter from those who do not share her understanding about the benefits of outdoor provision?*

- *How would Jenna answer these challenges, particularly when promoting children's choice of experiences?*

By enabling children to make choices, we acknowledge Article 12 of the United Nations Convention on the Rights of the Child (1989), which proposes that children have the right to express opinions and have their views acknowledged (Glazzard et al., 2010).

Reflecting on values and assumptions allows us to continually examine our views of childhood and preferential ways of working with children (Lancaster, 2010). This enables us to adapt our practice accordingly, which is an important aspect of pedagogical leadership. As an EYP, you should both recognise and articulate ways in which you interpret Early Years policy according to your knowledge of play and learning, your pedagogical approaches and the individual circumstances in which you carry out your role (S39). As you build up your evidence for your summative assessment, you are encouraged to think about how you demonstrate these pedagogical elements in your setting and, crucially, how you are supporting others to do this. Use the following task to support your thinking.

PRACTICAL TASK

'Take a creative and constructively critical approach towards innovation, and adapt practice if benefits and improvements are identified' S39 (CWDC, 2010a: 89)

Look at the statements in the first column, which relate to S39 and then add an example in the second column of how you could demonstrate these features of S39 in practice.

Table 5.2   Taking a critical approach to innovation

Statement (related to S39)	Example to show how this statement could be demonstrated in practice
Encourage colleagues to put forward their ideas	
Be open to innovative suggestions from others	
Consider innovations in a constructive manner	
Adapt practice if benefits and improvements are anticipated	

(Source: adapted from CWDC, 2010a: 89)

Pedagogical leadership: knowledge and experience

Details of the knowledge and understanding which enable EYPs to lead and support practice are found in S1–S6; for example, S2 is concerned with individual and different ways in which children learn and develop (CWDC, 2010a). However, your knowledge and understanding should be informed by a range of factors, including your wider reading, experiences, interactions with other professionals and people in your setting. As a pedagogical leader, your judgements and decisions about your own and others' practice are supported by developing a broad and deep knowledge and understanding of Early Years policy and practice, research outcomes and theoretical perspectives of children's learning and development (CWDC, 2010a).

An association between good outcomes for children and highly qualified practitioners (trained teachers), was established by the Effective Provision of Pre-school Education (EPPE) study (Sylva et al., 2004). We have already made reference to this significant longitudinal study, which examined the effects of pre-school education and care on children's learning and development. One of the key findings from the EPPE study suggested that one of the features of effective settings was the presence of practitioners who had good curriculum knowledge and understanding of ways in which children learn, provided a strong educational focus in the setting and supported less qualified practitioners (Siraj-Blatchford, 2010).

The EPPE study's definition of Early Years Pedagogy reflects an emphasis on interactions traditionally associated with the term 'teaching'; pedagogy is *the full set of instructional techniques and strategies that enabled learning to take place in early childhood that provided opportunities for the acquisition of knowledge, skills, attitudes and dispositions.*

(Siraj-Blatchford, 2010: 149)

The importance of practitioners' professional knowledge, which was established by EPPE, has contributed to an increased emphasis on professional development of staff within the Early Years sector in recent years, including the establishment of the graduate level EYPS (Sylva, 2010b). An EYP reflects on the beneficial effect of the development of her knowledge and understanding in the case study below.

CASE STUDY

Menna, EYP and sessional manager offering sessional care

'The research I have undertaken has influenced my practice and that in my setting. My main area of interest is the learning that takes place in child-initiated play. I firmly believe that the quality of children's learning is dependent on the quality of the continuous provision and know that I think more carefully about this in my setting. Such considerations, as well as my reflective nature, have undoubtedly made me a more effective practitioner. I also ensure that I understand the reasons for and research behind the new initiatives that are presented to the sector so that I understand how they will benefit the children in the setting. I have tried to ensure that new initiatives and changes are introduced clearly to all staff and that they have the opportunity to voice any concerns they may have.'

REFLECTIVE TASK

Reflecting on Menna's experiences, consider ways in which you think she perceives the development of her knowledge and understanding about child-initiated play and how that might:

- *impact on children's learning and development;*
- *impact on staff in her setting;*
- *support reflection and evaluation of her practice.*

Then select an area of practice that you have researched; for instance, 'transitions'. Reflect on how the development of your knowledge and understanding of this subject impacts on:

- *your developing role of pedagogical leadership;*
- *children's learning and development;*
- *parents' and carers' learning.*

A knowledge base, however, cannot remain static. Using the colourful analogy of the turn of a kaleidoscope, Robinson (2008) advises that knowledge about children's growth and change is of a 'fluid nature' because research continually provides us with fresh insights, such as emergent discoveries from research on brain development. Absorbing and applying new information is a complex task and, in your role as a pedagogical leader, you will be required to assimilate and understand a body of changing professional knowledge, in addition to that acquired through your everyday experiences. EYPs should seek out opportunities to engage in further professional development, alongside their role in leading practice in their setting (S38). This process is designed to ensure that EYPs remain informed about the latest changes to policy and practice and is addressed further in Chapter 9.

EYPs should be confident in their own understanding and be able to articulate their knowledge and experience to others, especially as they could be challenged in their role as pedagogical leaders. Barnett (2008: 192) contends that in a knowledge society 'everyone is knowledgeable' to some extent or can quickly update themselves on topics; therefore, professional knowledge could be challenged. However, S24 identifies that EYPs should be accountable in their setting and consider challenge to their views and ideas as an opportunity to reflect on their practice (CWDC, 2010a). Challenge, therefore, enables professionals to question their work and focus on the continuous adjustment of their pedagogic practices (Peeters and Vandenbroeck, 2011). The process of engaging with diverse views of Early Years practice can reveal new possibilities for mutual meaning-making (Claxton and Carr, 2004) and enables practitioners to develop an active and collective construction of knowledge (Siraj-Blatchford and Manni, 2007). By drawing on different forms of expertise, EYPs can develop 'relational agency': this is our capacity to 'learn from, learn about and learn with others' so expertise is continually redefined (Cable and Miller, 2011: 158). The following task enables you to consider opportunities for your learning and reflect on how your knowledge base is constructed, developed and redefined.

REFLECTIVE TASK

Reflecting on the specific context of your role, consider how you:

- *draw on a collective knowledge-base;*
- *are ready, willing and able to engage with new ideas and learn from others;*
- *accept that there are multiple ways of seeing and doing;*
- *appreciate that expertise is more than a body of specified knowledge and skills.*

(Adapted from Cable and Miller, 2011: 159)

If practitioners develop their understanding of the ways in which they support children's learning they are better equipped to tackle competing demands, critically evaluate new approaches, and positively impact on children's experiences (Stephen, 2010).

Pedagogical leadership: applying knowledge to practice

EYPs promote effective provision that is focused on improving children's outcomes by supporting practitioners to develop and apply their knowledge to practice, enabling new information to shape its development. By encouraging collaborative dialogue about children's learning and promoting critical reflection on practice and effective provision, you can enable colleagues to seek shared pedagogical understanding (Siraj-Blatchford and Manni, 2007). You can, therefore, exercise your pedagogical leadership by supporting practitioners to identify an 'informed responsive action' (Anning and Edwards, 2010: 242).

Practitioners' understanding can be facilitated, too, by pedagogical leaders working alongside colleagues; for instance, to demonstrate a different technique of observing children that will inform effective provision for a child's individual needs (S34). A commitment to provide respectful support and professional development opportunities for staff was identified as a feature of effective leadership of Early Years practice by the ELEYS study (Siraj Blatchford and Manni, 2007). Examples of these aspects of EYPs' leadership of practice are demonstrated in the following case studies.

The case studies below demonstrate some ways in which EYPs demonstrate their pedagogical leadership by extending their own knowledge and understanding and enabling their colleagues to develop and apply knowledge to their practice.

CASE STUDY

Fiona, an EYP and children's centre manager

'I have always endeavoured to study to continually improve myself and my setting. Through the initial stages of the Foundation degree, I found that gaining an understanding of child development theory and brain development aided my understanding of curriculum and children's learning. EYPS provided a thorough basis for practice through every element of leading a setting. As I was already leading a setting, I feel that EYPS was a consolidation of evidence to acknowledge my current practice; however, it also helped to confirm areas of strength and allowed reflection on the areas for future development. For without the opportunities to learn, reflect and evaluate practice, how can we develop and grow?'

CASE STUDY

Allana, an EYP and manager of a private nursery

'EYPS highlighted the importance of "reflective space" for all practitioners. I have undertaken a significant project to review the key person approach to facilitate smoother transitions for children in my setting. I have provided training for all staff on the implications of attachment theory for the key person approach.'

Nancy, an EYP and a childminder

'Undertaking EYPS has reminded me about what "I" did as an individual rather than as a team, which has demonstrated the knowledge I had. I have definitely become more confident in sharing what I have learned with others – for example, I encouraged a student on placement in my setting to think from the child's point of view. I find that by explaining a new way of working helps me to embed the knowledge in my mind. I have been very fortunate that my local authority has an EYP Network in place and I have attended training as part of a project on outdoor play. Children have had wonderful experiences exploring and investigating the local environment and I have been inspired by involving them in the planning process.'

Reflecting on the case studies above, consider how you share knowledge about aspects of Early Years practice to support the practice of others.

Although The Study of Pedagogical Effectiveness in Early Learning (SPEEL) (Moyles et al., 2002) pre-dates the introduction of both EYPS (2006) and the EYFS (2007), it is entirely concerned with effective pedagogical practice. In the task below, you are encouraged to consider how SPEEL conceptualised Early Years Pedagogy and this should aim to assist you in constructing your own understanding of this term.

Pedagogy is both the behaviour of teaching and being able to talk about and reflect on teaching. Pedagogy encompasses both what practitioners actually DO and THINK and the principles, theories, perceptions and challenges that inform and shape it. It connects the relatively self-contained act of teaching and being an Early Years educator, with personal, cultural and community values (including care), curriculum structures and external influences. Pedagogy in the early years operates from a shared frame of reference (a mutual learning encounter) between the practitioner, the young child and his/her family.

The definition above of Early Years pedagogy in the SPEEL study has been separated into four parts in the table below. Looking at each part in turn, add examples from your experience of practice that match the particular aspect of the definition in each quadrant. You might wish to discuss your examples with a colleague or your mentor.

Table 5.3 Aspects of Early Years pedagogy

Behaviour of teaching* and being able to talk about and reflect on teaching.	What practitioners actually DO and THINK and the principles, theories, perceptions and challenges that inform and shape these actions.
Connecting the relatively self-contained act of teaching and being an Early Years educator, with personal, cultural and community values (including care), curriculum structures and external influences.	Operating from a shared frame of reference (a mutual learning encounter) between the practitioner, the young child and his/her family.

* 'Teaching' can be interpreted here as any appropriate interaction between a practitioner and child that involves learning.

(Source: adapted from Moyles et al., 2002: 5)

SPEEL found that effective pedagogy is characterised by 'informed thinking', which is the 'conscious processes of interpretation and reflection and their application to practice' (Moyles et al., 2002: 120). This view of effective pedagogy is acknowledged too in EYFS guidance on good practice; practitioners are advised that:

> The more we are aware of our practices – what we do, why we do it, its impact on children and learning – and the more we reflect, learn and develop our practice, the more effective we will be. This is developing our pedagogy.

> (DCSF, 2009a: 4)

According to SPEEL, practitioners' capacity to be reflective is linked to their level of training and to an ethos which 'positively promotes self-evaluation and reflection and adopts strategies for developing these' (Moyles et al., 2002: 130). As we discussed in the last chapter, the process of 'reflection' is critical to your role as pedagogical leader; for instance, by using open questions about practice and the nature of its impact, you will encourage others in reflective thinking (DCSF, 2010a).

Pedagogical leadership: supporting pedagogical approaches

By carefully listening to and appreciating the values and interests of colleagues, parents and other relevant parties, as well as sensitively expressing your own standpoint on aspects of provision, you can establish, implement and review agreed pedagogical approaches to Early Years practice, which seek to promote good outcomes for all children. This is an important aspect of your pedagogical leadership; the task of identifying and articulating a collective vision, especially with regard to pedagogy and curriculum was acknowledged as an effective feature of leadership practice in the ELEYS study (Siraj-Blatchford and Manni, 2007). Sometimes, you will meet negative views from colleagues about an aspect of practice and your effectiveness as a leader will be shown in your awareness of these views, in anticipating reactions, thinking about causes of provocation and seeking possible solutions to resolve conflicting viewpoints and agree a way forward (DCSF, 2010a). Indeed, S33 calls for EYPs to develop a collaborative and cooperative culture with their colleagues and 'fair, respectful, trusting and constructive relationships' while S30 describes sensitive and effective communication with parents (CWDC, 2010a).

Play-based pedagogy

The EYFS demonstrates a fundamental commitment to play and playful learning; the framework requires that all areas of learning and development are 'delivered through planned, purposeful play, with a balance of adult-led and child-initiated activities' (DCSF, 2008a: 11).

The implications of this policy, though, are not that practitioners should *plan* children's play, as this would obstruct their opportunities for choice and control in play; practitioners should, rather, plan *for* play by developing 'high-quality learning environments' and opportunities for 'uninterrupted periods for children to develop their play' (DCSF, 2009a: 11). The pedagogical leader is, therefore, tasked with supporting the development of an enabling environment that is inspiring, challenging and imaginative and includes pedagogical approaches that support children's learning. Consider the examples of effective pedagogical approaches to play in the following task.

REFLECTIVE TASK

Reflecting on your own practice and your pedagogical leadership of others, consider how you:

- *ensure children have the opportunity to develop child-initiated activities;*
- *arrange and resource the environment appropriately and also ensure children can make free use of spaces;*
- *routinely observe children during all their activities;*
- *seek to understand children's thinking and learning, considering when to interact and when to listen;*
- *participate in children's play and child-initiated activity and follow the children's agenda;*
- *scaffold children's learning through talk, discuss ideas and strategies, suggest possibilities and model approaches;*

REFLECTIVE TASK CONTINUED

- *provide well-planned, brief, focused learning opportunities in response to children's observed interests, learning and development.*

(Adapted from DCSF, 2010a: 8–9)

While play is not the only mode of learning, Moyles (2010: 8) suggests that play is the 'essential pedagogical strategy to develop children's deeper learning'. The following task encourages you to provide examples of your provision 'for' play and ways in which play supports children's learning and development.

PRACTICAL TASK

In thinking about play, think of an example to demonstrate your commitment to playful learning.

Table 5.4 Play-based pedagogical strategies

Pedagogical strategy concerning play	Example to show how this strategy could be demonstrated in practice
Understanding of theoretical views that support the view of 'learning through play'	
Understanding of the reasons why play supports children's emotional and cognitive development	
Provision for children's freedom, choices and control in their play	
Provision of playful experiences	
Understanding of theoretical views that support the view of 'learning through play'	

(Source: adapted from Howard, 2010: 212)

References to effective pedagogical approaches cannot be viewed in isolation from other aspects of effective leadership of practice. There is, too, much potential for further research about the form and process of pedagogical approaches within Early Years practice, particularly with regard to developing an understanding of how these are applied effectively within the context of play (Broadhead et al., 2010).

We cannot leave this section, however, without reference to the Researching Effective Pedagogy in the Early Years (REPEY) study (Siraj-Blatchford et al., 2002) which evolved from the EPPE research and aimed to identify effective pedagogical strategies in Early Years practice. These studies have substantially informed our understanding of particular aspects of effective pedagogical approaches (Sylva et al., 2004) and their outcomes have been highly influential in shaping government policy (Miller and Pound, 2011). They have confirmed, for instance, the view that quality pre-school provision is significantly related to young children's language development, cognitive progress and social development (Sylva et al., 2006).

The EPPE study places an increased emphasis on the quality of the home learning environment which was found to have a more important effect on children's development than other significant influences such as parents' income, occupation or education (Siraj-Blatchford and Manni, 2007). This focus on high-quality pedagogical approaches requires all practitioners to reflect on how they support children's learning and development in the broadest sense; however, it has particular significance for the pedagogical leader who models practice and offers guidance to others. You are encouraged to explore further features of effective pedagogical approaches in the following Practical Task.

PRACTICAL TASK

Add examples of practice to these features of effective practice, which were identified by EPPE. Include any EYP Standards that apply to your example in the final column.

Table 5.5 EPPE and effective provision

Features of effective provison identified by EPPE	Your example of practice	Linked EYP Standards
Instructive learning environments and routines		
Provision of both adult-initiated group work and freely chosen play activities		
Promotion of sustained–shared thinking		
Children's cognitive and social development are treated as complementary and equally valid processes		
Formative feedback provided to children during activities		
Children supported to adhere to behaviour policies and discuss conflicts		

Table 5.5 Continued

Features of effective provison identified by EPPE	Your example of practice	Linked EYP Standards
Provision of differentiated learning opportunities that address the needs of groups and individual children		
Practitioners have strong engagement with parents and share educational aims		

(Adapted from Siraj-Blatchford, 2010: 161)

The growing body of research concerning children's learning and development has highlighted the unexpected competencies of very young children. These findings present a departure from previous theorisations about children's more limited competencies at the earliest stages of their development (Bowman et al., 2000) and have much relevance to pedagogical approaches to practice. For example, if very young children have sophisticated thinking skills and creativity, which are not acknowledged or valued by practitioners, their unique strengths, interests and aptitudes could go unrecognised (DSCF, 2010b). Therefore, as a pedagogical leader, you can support practitioners to be observant of children's competencies, even if these are not entirely apparent and to provide a broad range of experience, which engages and motivates children, supports their all-round development and acknowledges that all children have strengths. For example, consider how you could support practitioners with the following types of provision that take account of children's different competencies, needs and interests.

Consider how you could support practitioners to provide:

- *sufficient opportunities for children to be deeply involved, experiment and explore new lines of enquiry, represent their thinking and solve problems;*

- *an inspiring environment that provides provocations for learning that seek to capture children's imaginations;*

- *quiet spaces where children can ponder and play, as well as larger open spaces for them to explore new physical skills.*

(Adapted from DCSF, 2008e: 21)

CHAPTER SUMMARY

By exploring Early Years pedagogy in this chapter, we have seen that the role of pedagogical leadership is complex. Early Years pedagogy was first contextualised and some definitions of the term have been offered to support your thinking about this subject. You have been encouraged to form your own definition of Early Years pedagogy by considering various domains of the subject. This definition will help your understanding of the role of pedagogical leadership, which is highly dependent on the context of your role and setting.

We have considered how Early Years practice is shaped by different values and beliefs and understanding of policy and practice and discussed how pedagogical leaders keep informed about policy change and the findings of research studies that are concerned with young children's learning and development. They also support others to develop and apply knowledge and understanding about effective Early Years provision and develop effective pedagogical approaches. The relationship between policy and practice is not readily articulated or understood by all those involved in Early Years provision and the pedagogical leader cannot, for instance, provide a 'Satnav' guide to Early Years practice (Broadhead et al., 2010: 182). However, the common features of the EYP's role of pedagogical leadership are to demonstrate effective personal practice and to support and enable practitioners to provide appropriately for young children in their care and make a positive difference to their well-being, learning and development.

Moving on

We have already begun to identify the importance of the EYP in setting a vision for effective pedagogical practice and, in the next chapter, we focus on one of the defining elements of the EYP role, that of the 'catalyst of change' (CWDC, 2010a). We consider the development of skills in managing and leading change and understanding some of the factors that can impact on the change process. This will include reflections on strategies to overcome resistance to change through visionary leadership.

FURTHER READING

Allen, S. and Whalley, M. E. (2010) *Supporting Pedagogy and Practice in Early Years Settings*. Exeter: Learning Matters (Chapter 2: Perspectives on Early Years Pedagogy and Chapter 3: Children's Learning and Development).

Moyles, J., Adams, S. and Musgrove, A. (2002) *The Study of Pedagogical Effectiveness in Early Learning (SPEEL)* Research Report 363. London: DfES. Available at http://www.education.gov.uk/publications//eOrderingDownload/RR363.pdf

Siraj-Blatchford, I. (2010) A focus on pedagogy: case studies of effective practice. In Sylva, K., Melhuish, E., Sammons, P., Siraj-Blatchford, I. and Taggart, B. *Every Childhood Matters: Evidence from the Effective Pre-School and Primary Education Project*. London: Routledge.

6 The leader of practice as an agent of change

CHAPTER OBJECTIVES

In this chapter, we explore in more detail the concept of the EYP as one who can 'effect change' in order to 'improve outcomes for children' (CWDC, 2010a: 7) and set this in the context of the wider changes that are taking place within the Early Years workforce. Our focus here is to consider principles of change management and some of the factors that can either facilitate or hinder the effectiveness of changes to practice within the EYFS. In particular, through case studies and reflective exercises you will have opportunity to think about your own skills and areas for development in this key aspect of the EYP role.

After reading this chapter you should be able to:
- reflect on the theory and principles of change management and how to apply these to practice within the EYFS;
- critically appraise your own strengths and areas for development in your role in effecting change;
- apply your understanding to the preparation of your evidence for EYP validation.

This chapter is wide-ranging and will help you in your preparation of evidence against many of the standards and should be particularly helpful as you prepare your written tasks.

Introduction

As human beings we have an ambivalent attitude to change. We tend to be both resistant to it and, at the same time, strangely impelled by it. Change and adaptation have been crucial for human survival and, within organisations too, informed change is essential for success. Change, then, is both an inevitable and necessary part of our lives as individuals, professionally and within wider society. This is not to imply that most of us will find change easy, nor that change should be approached without any critical thought; but it does highlight the need for openness to new ways of understanding and of 'doing' practice. In the EYP role, you will need to model a positive but intelligent attitude to changes to practice, to understand some of the underlying causes of resistance to change and to apply some of the principles of change management to your role in effecting change.

The changing context of Early Years practice and provision

Whether you have worked in Early Years for many years or are a Full Pathway candidate to EYPS who is relatively new to the sector, you will be aware of something of the tidal wave of change that has swept through the children's workforce over recent decades in the form of new directions in policy and workforce reform. This is a global phenomenon and not limited to the UK (Oberheumer and Scheryer, 2008) and is ongoing. At the time of writing, while there is still much uncertainty within the UK, there are some encouraging indicators, not least in the Children's Minister's announcement that the Government will continue to invest in Early Years graduate programmes (Teather, 2011). Indeed, key findings from a recent survey indicate for the first time the positive impact of graduate-level training on the skills, status and on-going professional development of Early Years practitioners (Centre for Developmental and Applied Research in Education (CeDARE), 2011). The Tickell Review of the Early Years Foundation Stage Framework (Tickell, 2011) makes a number of key recommendations but time will tell exactly what shape the changes to EYPS will take.

'Change', then, can be said to be the one constant in Early Years! Arguably, the overall aim of this significant process of change in the sector has been the movement towards increased professionalism and the ensuing impact on the quality of provision for young children and their families. In seeking to achieve EYPS, you are part of this ongoing movement and so your role as 'catalyst of change' is particularly apt within this wider context.

Change management

Any search engine will identify literally thousands of references to strategies and programmes for managing change effectively within an organisation. This is indicative of just how key to 'success' the process of change management is. Your aim, as an EYP, is to make an active and informed contribution to effective practice within your setting so it is helpful if you know a little about the theory of change management. This will enable you to reflect on how you can apply this to your own role as a 'change agent'. Caution is needed, of course, as some of the strategies and programmes available can appear to suggest a 'quick fix' and over-simplified approach. Aspects of practice covered in previous chapters are relevant here; and emotional intelligence and strong interpersonal skills are critical in any approach to change.

Nevertheless, there are some insights from the wider literature that help us to understand something of the process of change, including factors that will facilitate or hinder it. One of the most helpful things we can do is to reflect on our own attitudes and responses to change in our lives – personally and/or professionally. Often, in the EYP role, you will find yourselves needing to introduce and lead on changes to practice that your colleagues might not choose for themselves. It is helpful, then, to try to put yourself in their shoes and reflect on what this might feel like for them. We know that change can have a considerable impact on the human mind: it can be 'threatening', especially when it is perceived as making a situation worse than at present; or it can be 'inspiring' because it offers the possibility of making a situation better (Whitney M. Young Junior, cited in Dickerson, 2004: 23).

REFLECTIVE TASK

The context *of change is important. Think now how you have reacted to change within your professional role that has been forced on you by circumstances beyond your control. Then, contrast this to your response to change that you have personally opted to make in your professional capacity. Make notes on the differences in your feelings and responses here. Do these help you to understand how colleagues might be feeling about some of the changes to practice you are introducing?*

Hersey and Blanchard (1988) describe the three stages of change management as:

- Diagnosis – of the situation, including the ability to make decisions based on sound judgement, which is fundamental to the EYP role (CWDC 2007).

- Adaptation – where practical steps are taken and an action plan put in place to work towards the changes.

- Communication – ensuring that all involved are consulted and listened to, kept informed and included in ongoing review of the changes.

This makes change management sound rather simple and formulaic but, of course, at each stage there are potential pitfalls. Sometimes there are errors in analysis of a situation; occasionally the plan of action is not realistic or is insufficiently detailed. Perhaps most importantly, communication can break down or fail to take full account of individuals' points of view and feelings.

In his 1976 children's poem, *A March Calf*, Ted Hughes describes the early experience of a newborn calf: 'A little at a time, of each new thing, is best. Too much and too sudden is too frightening' (Hughes, 2005). This can be seen to apply to most people and situations. The pace and timing of change can be crucial to its success. Straker (2010) helps us to understand something of the psychology of change and describes the importance of planning for change thoughtfully and carefully, through understanding the people who will be involved (both those engaged in the change and those who will feel the consequence of it), understanding the specific tasks involved and building the plans to bring about the change systematically and methodically.

We have already noted the two ways at looking at change, either with fear and anxiety or seeing the positive benefits of it. Resistance can come in many forms: active or passive; overt or covert: individual or organised; aggressive or timid (Straker, 2010). It is fear and anxiety that are at the roots of resistance but this can be masked in many forms, including overt comments such as: 'I like things the way they are', 'It could involve a lot more work' or 'I've been through too many changes already'. However, resistance can be less overt, even passive, with gossip and grumbling behind the scenes, colleagues not carrying out the tasks allotted to them, negative body language and even staff absence. Collective or organised resistance is one of the most challenging forms to face, where there is a common voice articulating objection to the proposed change.

The most effective ways of dealing with resistance involve active listening, empathy for the other's position and perspective, negotiation of the actual extent and timing of the change and offering support, guidance and training to facilitate colleagues' involvement in it. Eaton (2006) suggests a focus on the positive benefits of the change which should lead to more efficient work practices, greater success, the avoidance of stagnation and being seen as at the 'cutting edge' of good practice. Such aspirations are at the heart of the EYP role, to which we now turn our attention as we seek to apply some of these insights to the Early Years context.

The role of the EYP in effecting change

In the task of leading practice, there will inevitably be changes to introduce; indeed, from the outset the role of the EYP was promoted as that of 'agent of change' (Lee, 2010). We reflect for a few moments on this concept.

REFLECTIVE TASK

Look at these two definitions:

Change agent: a person whose presence or thought processes cause a change from the traditional way of handling or thinking about a situation.

(Barron's Banking Dictionary, 2010)

Change agent: someone who alters human capability or organizational systems to achieve a higher degree of output or self-actualisation.

(Stevenson, 2008)

- *How do you see such definitions applying to your role as an EYP?*

- *Much of your evidence for EYPS validation is based on your work as a 'catalyst for change'. Take this opportunity to begin to identify some of the opportunities and challenges you have in this aspect of your role.*

From her research, Rodd (2006) identifies a variety of types of change at different levels in early childhood settings: *incremental, induced, routine, crisis, innovative* and *transformational.* As an EYP, you could be involved with any one of these but the focus of your leadership role lies in induced and innovative change. Induced change stems from a conscious decision that some aspect of practice relating to people or processes needs to be changed; for instance, the reorganisation of a key person system in a setting. In innovative change, the leader seeks to introduce new practices in order to further the overall mission of a setting; such as changes to the way a programme is planned, using the children's own interests rather than a thematic approach.

We discussed the issue of resistance to change in the previous section and, for you in your role, one of the most determining success factors in the implementation of change will be the level of support or resistance from the staff involved. A good question to ask yourself, then, is: Why do some people demonstrate such resistance and appear to sabotage projects or planned change? Within Early Years, there are many complex reasons for this, including misunderstandings of the purpose of the change, lack of trust in the leader, lack of knowledge, fear of new technologies, differing personal value stances about Early Years practice, experience of excessive change and self-interest (based on Rodd, 2006: 189). In order to support staff in the change process, Schrag et al. (1985, cited in Rodd, 2006) suggest the following six 'C's of change:

- **Challenge**: aim to creatively turn perceived 'threats' into a positive challenge.

- **Communication**: consult widely and regularly with all staff, keeping them informed throughout the process.

- **Commitment/Collaboration**: encourage shared ownership of the change and try to avoid any suggestion that this is being 'imposed'.

- **Control**: allow all staff to feel that they are sharing in control of shape and pace of any change.

- **Confidence**: encourage resilience and self-confidence in staff.

- **Connection**: promote networks of support, both within a setting and from outside agencies where helpful.

REFLECTIVE TASK

- *Can you think of examples of both induced and innovative change in which you have led practice?*

- *From the six 'C's above, are you able to identify factors that contributed to either the success or lack of success in supporting this change?*

The agent of change as 'creative leader'

A further 'C' might be added to Schrag et al.'s list. The effective agent of change needs to be a *creative* leader. As Edgington states (2004: 8), the leader with creativity and imagination will demonstrate an 'optimistic disposition . . . a "can do" approach', showing that with ingenuity and persistence anything can be made to happen. The leader of practice has to be a 'possibility thinker', willing to *un*learn the tendency to follow conventional patterns and make predictable responses and develop innovative but workable approaches to all aspects of practice. This will involve the 'integration of your *expertise* with *experience* in order to bring a creative approach to problem-solving' (Isaksen and Tidd, 2006: 142); thus, to hold your professional expertise with your professional experience in balanced tension. Such an approach requires creative intelligence. It includes navigating change to ensure its successful achievement rather than resulting in acrimony or failure. More than this, when you apply creative intelligence to your leadership role you are providing the energy to overcome any inertia within your colleagues or setting. Look at the following case study and reflect on how Aliana is acting as a change agent in this situation.

CASE STUDY

When Aliana, EYP and lead practitioner in the pre-school room of a private nursery, wanted to introduce greater flexibility to the free-flow provision inside and out of the setting for the children, she met with a lot of resistance from the staff team. They insisted the present system worked well, staff rotas were manageable and because all the children went out at the same time, this meant that there was a higher staff:child ratio when the children were outside. From Aliana's value stance, and based on her knowledge and understanding of effective Early Years pedagogy, however, the present system was intrusive and the children had to stop in the middle of play situations and get ready to go outside at the scheduled time in the morning and afternoon sessions, with their outdoor play similarly interrupted when it was time to go back indoors. Aliana carried out some observations of the children so she had data to share with the staff. She then used a team meeting to outline the rationale for, and details of, her vision for a free-flow approach to the pre-school provision and appealed to the staff to introduce the system two days a week for a month and then meet again to review. Aliana listened carefully to colleagues' objections but was firm that this change was going to take place and discussed with staff the most manageable way for staff deployment, encouraging them to be vigilant to the choices the children themselves made about where to play. She stressed that it was important that staff join or observe their key children whenever possible, whether indoors or out. At the end of the month, the staff had seen for themselves that the children's play was no longer disrupted and offered positive feedback to Aliana about how the new system had enabled them to have quality time with some of their key children both indoors and out.

REFLECTIVE TASK

Identify ways in which Aliana balanced her professional expertise here with the importance of working with the staff team and all their concerns (experience). Why was she so successful here? Can you think of an opportunity you have had to balance your expertise with your current experience?

We see here again the concept of the Early Years setting as a 'community of learners' (Wenger, 1998) and are reminded that creative leadership involves 'intense learning' for the leader as well as those being led (Isaksen and Tidd, 2006: 143). This involves adding *new* knowledge to existing expertise and experience, an openness to new ways of thinking and a solution-focused approach to all the challenges of practice. As an EYP, you will require a high degree of emotional resilience and the need to be resourceful and imaginative in the approach taken. Look at how Jilly has led change in her setting.

CASE STUDY

Jilly is an EYP in the preparatory department of an independent school. She works with the class teacher and together they offer pre-school provision for 16 children aged 3–4 years. Having recently completed an early childhood studies degree as part of her 'journey' towards EYPS, Jilly underwent a radical change to her own understanding of early learning and development. The traditional practice in the department was to have fairly formal 'literacy' and 'numeracy' sessions each morning with the children. These were carried out in two groups of eight children, with one member of staff using a white board and other resources to 'teach' the children about letters, sounds and numbers. Through her own study, research and reflections, Jilly's personal beliefs and values altered and she began to feel increasingly uncomfortable with this approach. She broached this first with the class teacher and suggested that they embed opportunities for children to learn about letters, sounds and numbers, in a more focused way, within the continuous and enhanced provision in the setting. The teacher was reluctant at first but having read research journal articles which Jilly shared with her, agreed to let Jilly make some small changes to practice which included providing mark-making opportunities in the role-play area and clipboards outside. She also introduced counting games and those involving number recognition – indoors and out. The time spent in the formal group activities was reduced gradually. However, when parents learned of this, they objected as they believed the children were 'not making enough progress' in writing and counting skills. The class teacher suggested Jilly set up a Parents' Workshop at which they presented to parents some of the positive benefits of developmentally appropriate play-based learning. An evaluation of the workshop by parents indicated that most parents had been convinced about the value of the changes.

REFLECTIVE TASK

- *How does Jilly apply creative leadership in this situation?*

- *What strategies has she used to overcome resistance to the changes she believed were important?*

- *Can you think of two examples when you have used a similarly creative approach to leadership in your own setting?*

The agent of change as 'visionary leader'

We have noted previously Rodd's (2006) and Moyles' (2006) work on defining the role of the leader as visionary and influential. Clearly, the ability to define and articulate a vision for practice within your Early Years setting is a crucial aspect of your EYP leadership role. Your vision will stem from your personal value stance, your personal reflections on the direction of travel of Early Years policy, your personal commitment to your own learning, your wider reading of the theoretical literature and your contextual knowledge of your immediate setting. Each of these aspects is important. As part of your role as 'visionary leader' you will introduce to practice any necessary *information* and *expertise* from this wider context. However, Smith and Langston (1999: 20) remind us that, as leaders, we should be 'realistic' as well as visionary, show sensitivity to others in the way we lead and be 'practical' as well as innovative.

CASE STUDY

Linda, EYP, is the manager of a full day nursery. As such she is usually the first point of contact for the setting: for parents, other professionals and statutory bodies, etc. Over recent months, Linda has been involved in leading practice on improving the nursery's approach to:

- *planning for the under-threes to take full account of the EYFS framework;*

- *introducing a healthy eating menu and making changes to the snack time provision for the preschool children (cafeteria style);*

- *behaviour management, including encouraging the children to create their own ground rules;*

- *communication with parents through the establishing of open afternoons at weekends with emphasis on a particular aspect of learning/development – such as communication, language and literacy;*

- *Staff's competence in using ICT to support teaching and learning.*

REFLECTIVE TASK

All these are aspects of practice, so although Linda also has primary responsibility for managing the organisation of her setting, she is also the lead practitioner. Think about the information and expertise that Linda has needed in order to lead on these – demonstrating practicality as well as innovative practice. Begin to reflect on the way you access key information and acquire the expertise required for you to lead change in your own setting.

Walden and Shiba (2001) outline eight principles for the visionary leader and while not all these are directly applicable to you as EYP, they do offer some important insights into the role, especially in leading change. Their principles are adapted here with some questions which offer you a tool with which you can appraise your own practice as a visionary leader.

REFLECTIVE TASK

Table 6.1 Principles of visionary leadership

Walden and Shiba's (2001) principles of visionary leadership	Application to your own leadership practice
Principle 1 The visionary leader is observant and vigilant and must do on-site observation leading to personal perception of changes in societal values. **EYP role:** Here the role of the leader in empowering staff by keeping them fully informed of key changes affecting policy and practice is emphasised. This includes staff changing their own perceptions and value stance.	In what ways do you act as a conduit of key information relating to policy and practice matters in your setting?
Principle 2 Even though there is resistance, the visionary leader never gives up; squeezing the resistance between outside-in pressure in combination with top-down inside instruction. **EYP role:** Here the often precarious role of the leader is stressed; this involves translating and making many of the changes 'manageable' and 'doable' to/by staff.	Can you think of an instance when your vision for practice was met with resistance by colleagues? What helped you to stick with your vision here?
Principle 3 The visionary leader begins transformation of practice with symbolic disruption of the old or traditional system, through top-down efforts to create chaos within the organisation. **EYP role:** The role of the leader in being able to deal positively and effectively with the chaos is an inevitable part of transition from one way of organising/'doing' practice and another.	Think of an instance when you have been involved in leading change to practice. What personal coping strategies do you have to enable you to cope with the chaos of transition and retain your sense of vision?
Principle 4 The direction of visionary transformation is illustrated by a symbolic visible image and the visionary leader's symbolic behaviour. **EYP role:** Shared action planning and positive role modelling – not just in behaviour but by attitude – are crucial factors in successful visionary transformation.	Think further of the instance above. How did you convey by both action and attitude your positive approach to change?

Walden and Shiba's (2001) principles of visionary leadership	Application to your own leadership practice
Principle 5 Quickly establishing new physical, organisational and behavioural systems is essential for successful visionary transformation. **EYP role:** This principle needs a note of caution! The management and timing of change is critical. New systems are indeed crucial but what is needed of the leader is to inspire confidence in colleagues and to empower them to play their part in implementing change. Getting the timing/timescale for this 'right' is a key leadership skill.	What organisational skills do you believe you bring to visionary leadership? Are there any you particularly need to develop? Can you think back to the time management aspect of the instance above? In retrospect, reflect on the appropriateness of this.
Principle 6 Real change leaders are necessary to enable transformation. **EYP role:** Skills in change management are essential for all leaders of practice.	Begin to reflect on your skills and areas for development in change management.
Principle 7 Create an innovative system to provide feedback from results. **EYP role:** In order to continuously encourage and support colleagues in changes to practice, it is important to build in regular opportunities for feedback, review and updates.	Think of the last time you created an action plan with colleagues in order to implement some aspect of change to practice. Did this include structured opportunity for review on a regular basis? If not, why not?
Principle 8 Create a daily operation system, including a new work structure, new approach to human capabilities and improvement activities. **EYP role:** This connects to the role of EYP as a leading reflective practitioner, encouraging colleagues to review their own practice and engage in an ongoing programme of continuing professional development (cpd).	How do you share with colleagues your own programme of cpd? In what ways do you role-model effective reflective practice on a daily basis?

(Source: adapted from Walden and Shiba, 2001)

Being an 'agent of change' in leading the delivery of the EYFS

Up to the mid-1990s, there was no regulated framework for early learning in the UK. Since then, we have seen a number of major changes, the latest being the introduction of the EYFS framework from 2008 (DCSF, 2008a). The role of EYP was viewed as critical to the successful delivery of the EYFS, though following a change of government in 2010, as we have seen, there will almost certainly be changes (Tickell, 2011). It is almost certain though that the fundamental principles and themes of the EYFS will remain the bedrock of good practice in the Early Years: a unique child, positive relationships, enabling environments and learning and development. These themes should be viewed holistically whenever you are addressing opportunities to effectively implement and/or introduce changes to practice in your setting. This principled approach to the EYFS is aimed at fulfilling the overarching aim of the framework, which is to help young children stay safe; be healthy; enjoy and achieve; make a positive contribution; and achieve economic well-being (DfES, 2003). Look at the following 'snapshots' of experiences from a range of EYPs who have sought to be agents of change in delivering the EYFS in their settings, and use the reflective questions to think about your own role and practice.

CASE STUDY

Kirsty, owner/manager of a private full-day care setting:

'I have always aimed to be child-centred in my practice. By this, I mean that we observe children systematically on a regular basis and use these observations to plan our programme, drawing on the children's interests. I have worked in and owned this nursery for eight years and worked hard to ensure that all our policies are updated regularly and accessible to staff and parents. I was particularly proud of our new Inclusion Policy, although in all the time I have worked here, we have not had a request for a place for any children with physical disabilities or medical conditions. When a mum approached us to register her two-year-old (non-identical) twins, one of whom has cerebral palsy and is not yet walking and the other who is hearing-impaired, I responded positively as now I felt we had opportunity to turn our policy into practice and demonstrate our commitment to the EYFS theme of "a unique child". Prior to the children starting, I worked with the staff team on understanding the particular needs of both the twins, appraising the toddler room and environment to see what changes we may need to make and thinking through the key person system here and the importance of close relationships with mum.'

Davyd, leader/supervisor of a pre-school department in an independent school setting:

'My setting is in a very rural area and the children who attend are either from families who have lived in these villages for generations or from incomers to our area. We are aware there is a little tension in the wider community between both "sets" of families – with some of the established families somewhat resentful about the perceived "changes" that the incomers have made to village life. I believe that in our school we can model "positive relationships", one of the themes of the EYFS. We do this as a staff team and we encourage healthy social development with the children – both in their relationships with us as adults and with each other. I introduced a system of parent helpers where, on two sessions each week, two parents volunteer to come in and support the programme in a variety of ways (baking, sewing, story-telling, box modelling and so on). So far, 12 of our parents have volunteered and so I have created opportunities for "established" and "newcomer" parents to work together on a rota on this. Each half term, we have an

evening where we meet with parents informally at the school, share light refreshments and discuss some aspect of our provision. It is really encouraging to see positive relationships developing in the parent group.'

Emma, owner/manager of a private full-day care setting:

'Since achieving EYPS, I have felt very much more confident in my role as leader of practice although I am still very careful to consult with my staff and listen to their viewpoints. While I realise that "change" is very challenging for some people, I believe we all share a common commitment to making our setting the best it can be for the children and families we serve. However, there has been an issue recently within the staff team, with my appointment of a new deputy manager from outside our setting. One of our regular staff, Millie, also applied for the post but I am confident I made the right appointment and Shazia, new deputy, is generally settling in well. Millie was quite abrupt in her relationship with Shazia at first and tended only to respond tersely when Shazia asked her about an aspect of practice. I recognised that, if unaddressed, this situation could intensify and Millie become overtly or covertly resistant to any innovative practice that Shazia and I wanted to introduce. Millie is a very good practitioner and so I felt I needed to meet with her and address this situation directly with her. Millie expressed her feelings of disappointment and resentment about the interview but also recognised that her own negative reactions were unhelpful to everyone, including the children. We worked on a specific area of responsibility that Millie might take on and she suggested that she develop the use of empathy dolls which we had been considering purchasing for the setting.'

Wynette, a registered childminder:

'At present, I just have two children to "mind": Nia, aged four, attends all five days but I take her to the local pre-school on three mornings, and James, aged 18 months, attends three full days so has three mornings when he is the only child I have. Nia has two afternoons on her own with me. I am fortunate to have a bespoke playroom in my home for my work, which is accessed from the kitchen and has direct access to a child-height toilet and washbasin and also leads into my fenced garden. I have worked hard this year to think about the learning environment I am creating in my home and am seeking to make it truly "enabling" for the children in my care. This has been a challenge, given the diverse needs and development stage of the two children I have at present but I was able to discuss with Nia, particularly, the resources she would like in the playroom and garden and discuss with James' mum his particular preferences and interests.'

Carolyn, manager of a private full-day care setting:

'My setting, catering for children aged two to five years, is situated on the edge of a small town, with the countryside not very far away. We have a very effective free-flow system in place and note that generally the majority of children spend more time outdoors than in so we know all areas of our environment are being well used. However, from my observations, I noted that the quality of engagement between the staff and children

varied considerably indoors and out, with many staff taking a passive, supervisory role outdoors while engaging more directly in the children's play indoors. From my own pedagogical base, I was concerned that they were a) not responding sufficiently to opportunities to develop children's learning outdoors and b) in danger of intervening and joining in too readily in the children's indoor play. I was able to use a series of three weekly staff meetings to discuss this with the staff and use different training strategies to strengthen their understanding and practice of their role as pedagogues.'

Dawn, leader/supervisor of parent committee-led pre-school setting:

'This year in pre-school, I have 15 boys and just five girls on the register so have had to reflect on the way I organise our environment and the provision I offer. I needed to guard against unhelpful stereotyping but, at the same time, make sure that I was genuinely offering a broad and balanced programme which would support the learning and development of all the children. Quite early on in the year, I observed that the majority of the boys were really "into" superhero play which involved a lot of imaginary play – hunting for treasure and "doing magic", as well as some rough and tumble play. I wanted to encourage this as I could see how absorbed the children were, the levels of expressive language they were using, etc. However, one of the consequences was that the girls were quite excluded; they made no attempts to join in the boys' play, the boys did not invite the girls to play and the girls' opportunities for imaginative play were focused solely on the "home corner" provision. One or two of the boys, likewise, were not part of the superhero play. I discussed this with the staff, some of whom likewise were concerned about this and together we worked on a number of changes to the way we organised the setting, especially in making circle time and other outdoor play activities more inclusive of the whole group.'

These EYPs are all demonstrating their capacity to reflect both 'in' and 'on' action (as we outlined in Chapter 4) and make decisions, based on sound and informed judgements, about changes that are needed to develop or improve practice. Reflect here on opportunities you have currently to change practice in order that:

- *your setting more effectively demonstrates commitment to 'a unique child';*

- *'positive relationships' in your setting (child–child; practitioner–child; practitioner–practitioner; practitioner–parent, etc.) are strengthened;*

- *the environment is used more effectively and in a way that 'enables' children to learn and develop;*

- *you and colleagues have a greater understanding of children's development and the underpinning pedagogical base for children's learning.*

C H A P T E R   S U M M A R Y

In this chapter, we have identified some of the essential skills and knowledge required by EYPs in their role as agents of change. In particular, skills in decision-making and competence in leading change using creative and visionary leadership styles have been highlighted. These all connect very clearly with EYP S38 and S39 where any approaches to innovation or changes to practice must be supported with skilled reflection and analysis both of the situation and of your own role. As leaders of practice, a confident approach to your role is vital as you develop skills in change management. However, it is important that you understand why some colleagues are resistant to change and can work positively with them to help them see the positive benefits of changes to practice.

Moving on

In the next chapter, many of the themes addressed in this chapter are developed as the focus shifts to partnership work. You have opportunity to learn about the importance of team work and some of the strategies aimed at ensuring that Early Years teams are maintained as well as built. We explore the principles of collaborative practice and the significance of social and emotional intelligence and reflect on how these are applied to the EYP's role in partnership with colleagues and with parents.

FURTHER READING

Johnson, P. (2010) Becoming an Early Years Professional. In Farrelly, P. (ed.) *Early Years Work-Based Learning*. Exeter: Learning Matters (Chapter 4).

Rodd, J. (2006) Initiating and implementing change. In *Leadership in Early Childhood*, 3rd edition. Buckingham: Open University Press (Chapter 10).

7   Leading in partnership with parents and colleagues

CHAPTER OBJECTIVES

In this chapter, we explore how the EYP can demonstrate leadership in partnership with others: with colleagues and with the families of the children in the setting. Here, leadership does not necessarily imply a 'team leader' role but, rather, the demonstration and practice of effective collaboration. We identify the importance of emotional and social intelligence in collaborative practice. We consider the importance of understanding team roles and factors that contribute to successful team work with colleagues. We also reflect on the key elements of partnership with parents. Through case study examples and reflective activities, you will have the opportunity to discern the importance of your role as a supportive leader of collaborative practice.

After reading this chapter you should be able to:
- discuss factors that contribute to effective teamwork;
- reflect critically on the importance of social and emotional intelligence;
- appraise critically your own strengths and areas for development in this area;
- apply your understanding to the preparation of your evidence for EYP validation.

This chapter focuses specifically on EYP Standards 29–32 and 33–35 but you are encouraged to reflect broadly across the other Standards as you seek to apply your knowledge, understanding and skills in partnership work to all aspects of your practice.

Introduction

In leading the Early Years Foundation Stage (EYFS), very few of you will work in isolation and the intention in this chapter is that you should focus on the 'collaborative' aspect of your role, even if you work in an isolated context most of the time. Most of you will be part of a team of colleagues and/or other professionals, all working together towards a common goal or outcome, that of providing the highest possible quality provision and practice for young children across the EYFS. Whether or not you work in a context with colleagues, you will all be engaged in partnership with families. One of the fundamental requirements for the leadership role in Early Years settings is a commitment to collaboration, where 'effective pedagogic and parental support are complementary' (Siraj-Blatchford and Manni, 2007: 12). Here, you will be able to draw on your experiences of some of the positive and more challenging experiences of collaborative practice.

First, we will consider briefly some of the relevant theoretical frameworks that apply to building effective teams and focus on the skills and attributes required by the EYP in leading practice in a team context, even when not in the explicit role of 'team leader'. We look, however, not just at the *formation* of strong teams but how these can be *maintained* over a period of time. Sometimes things go wrong in teams and we explore how the EYP might be alert to early indicators of difficulties and how s/he can support stronger relationships between team members, even in conflict situations.

Partnership with families is the second distinctive aspect of collaboration and, as an EYP, you will be expected to demonstrate respectful relationships with the families linked to your setting and to value their role in their children's learning. How you can lead others in this aspect of practice is the focus of the final part of this chapter.

Teams

What is a 'team'? Dictionary definitions all offer some variation of 'a number of persons associated in some joint action'. This is quite different from a 'group' which is simply a collection of individuals who happen to be in the same place at the same time but not necessarily bound by any common purpose. Stacey (2009: 12) reminds us that such common purpose is an essential element of any team, but to be effective 'all team members need an understanding of how they can contribute to achieve [a] common goal'.

Rodd's early research (1998) in England and Australia adds a further dimension to the definition of a team when applied to early childhood settings. She found the element of cooperation between team members to be significant, with the achievement of an agreed set of aims or goals balanced with 'consideration of the personal needs and interests of individuals within the team' (Rodd, 1998: 100).

Look at the following case studies and reflect on how these practitioners are describing their experiences of being part of team.

CASE STUDY

Rosie, EYP: room leader in the full-day care provision within a chidren's centre

'Each week all the room leaders meet with the manager for briefing and review. I make sure our room team meets prior to this and provide opportunity for colleagues to share any concerns or issues they wish me to take to the manager's briefing. At the meeting, the manager always encourages each of us to share our views and ideas. We each feel really valued by him and know he appreciates the way we share leadership with him.'

CASE STUDY

Toni, EYP: supervisor of a voluntary pre-school

'I have always been a highly energetic person with lots of drive and thought I was a good team leader. Our recent Ofsted inspection highlighted the strong leadership in the pre-

CASE STUDY CONTINUED

school. However, I overheard one of my staff saying that I didn't give them enough opportunity to make decisions but really just expected them to rubber-stamp my ideas. I didn't say anything immediately but reflected on this later and recognised my own reluctance to delegate. I questioned my own practice: did I not trust my staff's judgements?'

CASE STUDY

Rahana: childminder, preparing for EYPS validation

'It is not easy for me to think immediately in terms of working in a team but then I remember that each week, I take my minded children to the local childminders' network play session at the community centre. There we each take turns to lead the song and story session for all the children and usually discuss together different aspects of our practice. Last week, Sara wanted to know about my experiences with Salid, one of my minded children, who is two and a half and who is very inquisitive with lots of "why?" and "how?" questions, and some of the activities I plan for him. Sara has a new little girl starting with her who is a lot like that, too.'

REFLECTIVE TASK

- *What are the differences between these three teams in the case studies?*

- *In terms of team effectiveness, how critical is the way the leaders see their role?*

- *Can you see how Rosie, Toni and Rahana might use these reflections to support their evidence for S33, and for other Standards?*

Team formation

You may well be familiar with Tuckman's (1965) seminal work on team formation based on the fundamental principles that teams, like all other living organisms, go through different stages of development and are not static. The original Tuckman model had four linear stages, though Tuckman with Jensen (1977) later added a fifth. In reality, it is unlikely that these stages are as sequential as thus presented, and some teams will seem to spend longer in one stage and even miss one out altogether. However, it remains a useful model in helping us to understand team processes and Table 7.1 is an adaptation of Tuckman and Jensen's model where the dimension and challenges of leadership are considered (Isaksen and Tidd, 2006). Look at this and then complete the reflective task.

Table 7.1 Stages of team development

Stage	Characterised by	Leadership dimensions
1. FORMING (orientation towards team identity)	Uncertainty and anxiety about other team members and the tasks/goals	Possible over-dependence on you. Important to clarify the tasks, provide the structures and encourage confidence
2. STORMING	Interpersonal tension: possible conflict between team members – may be overt or covert	Facilitative leadership is required which acknowledges diversity and models effective and sensitive listening each to the other
3. NORMING	A sense of 'belongingness' is established with conflict resolved	Importance of leader recognising the group's success and rewarding this appropriately
4. PERFORMING	A growing sense of inter-dependence among team members and cooperation in task achievement; some risk-taking	Key leadership task is to keep the team on track but also allow them scope and autonomy in 'performance'
5. TRANSFORMING (sometimes also called ADJOURNING)	Task completed/goal achieved; celebration of success and of positive relationships formed mixed reactions to 'ending' of team or task	If team disbands, leader's role is to reflect on success and what can be learned from it and to provide appropriate 'ending'; if team is to continue on to new task, there may be new members to include and new goals to negotiate

REFLECTIVE TASK

Think of an opportunity you have had to work with a team on a project or innovation. Are you aware of the stages the team went through in this task? Reflect particularly on your experience of leading the beginning ('forming') and ending ('transforming') stages in this.

Team-building

The successful functioning of any team is dependent on each individual member functioning well, where each person acts as a kind of catalyst to the other. As we have seen already, EYP Standard 33 requires you to 'establish and sustain a culture of collaborative and cooperative working between colleagues' (CWDC, 2010a: 76) There are two elements here: the establishment of *building* of a team and then its *maintenance.*

99

Edgington (2004) suggests that there are three main types of team in Early Years settings:

- **the cosy team:** usually well established; members have worked together for a long time; systems and organisation works well for them; show a united hostility to new ways of working; not welcoming to new members; attitude to change is to ignore it;

- **the turbulent team:** on the surface all appears to be well; at meetings the majority accept the decisions of the few; but outside, strong disagreement/disquiet may be expressed behind the backs of those most vocal at meetings; change is difficult to effect because there is no clear dialogue for shared decision-making;

- **the rigorous and challenging team:** professional approach; outward looking with a strong commitment to continuing professional development; regular reviews of practice; do not always agree but will discuss issues critically and try to reach a consensus ; open to change but with a thoughtful, well-prepared approach; never fully satisfied with what they are doing and challenge each other.

REFLECTIVE TASK

- *Have you any experience of working in any such teams?*

- *Reflect on the positives and negatives of this experience.*

- *If you have experience of two types, what were the main differences in effectiveness?*

- *What are the particular challenges for the leader in each type of team?*

An internet search will identify literally thousands of references to 'team building' strategies, indicating how important these are to organisational success. Rodd (2006) suggests that there, in fact, two key dimensions involved in team building: staff morale and task demands. The role of the leader is to hold these two in tension, recognising that a task will not be achieved if members of staff feel uncertain of what is involved, are lacking in confidence or feeling under-valued. However, equally, the leader needs to hold fast to the achievement of the goal that has been identified and not be deflected from the task. Gillen (1995, cited in Smith and Langston, 1999: 44) describes four principles in the process of building a team:

- **pull, don't push** – allow the team, not the leader, to set the pace;

- **involve people as much as possible** – encourage the team to think through ideas and take ownership of them;

- **think behaviour rather than personality** – observe individual behaviours rather than labelling their actions;

- **persuade, don't manipulate** – respect the other person and try to see their point of view.

As an EYP, it is important that you apply some of these principles to your role as leader of practice. The work of Neugabauer and Neugabauer (1998, cited in Rodd, 2006: 163–64) is significant here. They offer a five-step framework for team-building in early childhood settings:

- **set achievable goals** – mutually agreed by all team members;

- **clarify and explain roles** – where individual roles are clear to all and free of conflict; the leader's role in identifying all the tasks required and individuals to undertake these is key here;

- **build supportive relationships** – developing trust and providing resources to develop a cooperative team spirit;

- **encourage active participation** – capitalise on the skills and knowledge of each team member;

- **monitor team effectiveness** – build in regular opportunities to assess goal achievement and teamworking.

Look at the following case study and consider how Debbie, an EYP and deputy manager of a private full-day care setting, might apply insights from theory to building the team in the Tinies' room.

CASE STUDY

'Although super-numerary for much of the time, I now spend around 50 per cent of my week working with the staff team in the Tinies' section, for babies from 6–18 months. All the staff are really committed and conscientious and the key person system is working well but I do feel that there is an over-emphasis on the babies' care needs with little priority given to their needs to learn and develop. The Tinies' room does have direct access to a small, secure outdoor area but currently this is not used regularly.'

REFLECTIVE TASK

How might Debbie apply the five-step approach (Neugabauer and Neugabauer, 1998) in her leadership role?

Group dynamics and roles within teams

The work of Meredith Belbin (1993) has been hugely significant in helping us understand the different roles required for effective team work. While Belbin's nine team roles fit more naturally into the arenas of business and commerce, they are useful in helping us see the complementary nature of the different roles within a team – where diversity is viewed as an opportunity and not a threat. Belbin describes each of the roles as essential while an effective balance between the different roles is key to success.

Critical to Belbin's theory is the concept that for each of the strengths a particular role brings to the team, there are also allowable weaknesses. Table 7.2 offers a summary of

Belbin's definitions of team roles and further details can be accessed at http://www.belbin.com/rte.asp?id=8. It is worth taking a moment here to reflect that one of the tasks of the leader of practice is to understand the individuality of each team member and to embrace diversity. The principles highlighted in Chapter 3 relating to equality practice with children and families apply equally to working with a diverse team of colleagues.

Table 7.2 Belbin's team roles

Team role	Contribution to teamwork	Allowable weakness
PLANT	Creative problem-solver	Can be over-focused and fail to communicate effectively
RESOURCE INVESTIGATOR	Enthusiastic explorer of opportunities; develops contacts/networks	Can be over-optimistic and lose interest when obstacles appear
COORDINATOR	Mature; confident; delegates; promotes decision-making	May be seen as manipulative
SHAPER	Challenging; dynamic; thrives on pressure; can overcome obstacles	Often hurts people's feelings; makes unthinking remarks
MONITOR EVALUATOR	Strategic and discerning; grasps overview of a situation and judges accurately	Lacks dynamism and the ability to inspire others
TEAM WORKER	Cooperative; listens; gets on with task; averts friction	Indecisive at crunch points
IMPLEMENTER	Disciplined; reliable and efficient; turns ideas into practice	Often inflexible and slow to respond to new ideas
COMPLETER FINISHER	Painstaking; conscientious; reliable; thorough	Inclined to worry unduly and reluctant to delegate
SPECIALIST	Single-minded; dedicated; provides specialist skills/knowledge	Makes contribution only on narrow front

---

REFLECTIVE TASK

Look again at the list of team roles, contributions to teamwork and their allowable weaknesses.

- *Do you recognise your own personal role in your team context?*

- *Can you identify others in your team who assume some of the other roles?*

- *What are the particular challenges for the EYP in leading practice within a team where each member brings both positive contributions and allowable weaknesses?*

As an EYP, you also need to take account of the dynamics within your team. These are generally defined as interactions between team members in such a manner that each person influences and is influenced by each other person (Shaw, 1976). The impact of positive dynamics is team cohesion, whereas when negative factors are in play these can undermine team effectiveness. The following 'S' factors can affect cohesion.

- **stability** – the longer the team is together with the same members, the greater the opportunity for cohesion;

- **similarity** – the more similar the team members are in terms of age, gender, skills and attitudes, the greater the cohesion;

- **size** – the larger the group, the more challenging cohesion becomes;

- **support** – the more effectively teams are led and managed, the greater the cohesion;

- **satisfaction** – cohesion is associated with the extent to which team members are pleased with each others' performance, behaviour and commitment to the common task.

(McCauley et al., 1998)

Consider the following two scenarios in two separate Early Years settings.

Setting 1: Jingles Nursery is a popular private provider of Early Years provision for children from three months to five years. Jo, the owner manager, has had overall responsibility for the nursery since it was established ten years ago and has built up strong rapport with her staff and with the families who use the nursery. There are 12 staff members altogether, half of whom have also been employed there since it opened. All members of staff are women and all have comparable Early Years qualifications, except for Suzi who joined the staff six months ago and who has a degree in childhood studies. Jo deals with all the day-to-day running of the nursery and there are prescriptive systems in place for planning, monitoring and reporting children's progress. There are three room leaders, one of whom is Suzi, and all are committed to high-quality practice. Suzi has recently decided to proceed to validation for EYPS.

Setting 2: Jangles Pre-School is a voluntary setting catering for the needs of children from two to five years. Jak, an EYP, is the new playleader and a number of staff have moved on since she arrived a year ago. Jak has found it hard to recruit qualified practitioners to replace those who have left and two new staff members tend to have very different ideas from Jak about practice while another lacks confidence and is very dependent on Jak for support and guidance.

REFLECTIVE TASK

- *What factors affect cohesion at Jingles Nursery? What are the particular leadership challenges faced by Jo and Suzi?*

- *What factors affect cohesion at Jangles Pre-School? What are the particular challenges facing Jak and the whole staff team there?*

Team effectiveness

The characteristics of an effective team can be summarised by a sense of common purpose and clear objectives; a workable balance of roles within the team; a shared and (mainly) equal commitment from all team members; and effective communication and dialogue within the team (Daly et al., 2004).

Clearly, an effective team is one where there is a high degree of satisfaction because the targets it sets itself are achieved. Rodd's (1998) research on the factors that contribute to job satisfaction within Early Years teams offers valuable insights here. As you read the list, you might like to think about your role in leading practice and your own contribution to team effectiveness:

- support and stimulation;

- a sense of belonging and equality;

- opportunity for growth and development;

- stress reduction;

- facilitation of a pleasant working environment;

- opportunity to work through issues and the minimalisation of conflict;

- the opportunity to role-model team effectiveness to children and families;

- the opportunities for all team members to take a lead role on some aspect of practice and provision;

- shared work load and mutual encouragement in the achievement of the common task;

- shared human resources, ideas and skills;

- acknowledgement of each member's professional capabilities.

One of your tasks as EYP is to maximise team effectiveness and identify and minimise any hindering factors that prevent successful teamwork, especially in leading the EYFS and in implementing change. Even where you are not officially in the role of team leader, within your responsibilities as a leader of practice it is important that you are able to analyse and evaluate the strengths and weaknesses of the team with whom you are working and seeking to lead. Isaksen and Tidd (2006: 185) refer to the 'assets and liabilities' of any team, which concurs with Belbin's work on the positive contributions and allowable weakness of each team member. The potential 'liabilities' and difficulties in teamwork are considered in the final section of this chapter but here we consider the potential strengths of teamwork, which include the following:

- greater availability of knowledge and information;

- more opportunity for shared thinking, thus increasing the likelihood of building and developing the ideas of others;

- a wide range of experiences, perspectives and (human) resources on which to draw;

- increased understanding and ownership of team outcomes drawn from participation and involvement in decision-making and problem-solving;

- opportunities for personal and professional development through increasing team cohesion, communication and companionship.

REFLECTIVE TASK

Think of opportunities you have in your current role in leading practice to nurture cohesion, communication and companionship between colleagues.

- *How might you model these aspects of teamwork more effectively?*

- *What impact do you believe effective teamwork has on the children's experiences?*

- *Can you link your reflection here to S33?*

We cannot leave discussion on team effectiveness without reflecting briefly on the variables identified by Burton and Dimbleby (1988) which can affect teams. These are person variables, environmental variables and task variables. Holding together the different abilities – and for the EYP this can often be expressed in the different levels of experience and training of the Early Years practitioners (Siraj-Batchford et al., 2002) – personality traits, motives and value stances of individual team members requires skilled leadership. Person variables may also include staff changes and the challenges of recruitment. The environmental variables include specific factors relating to the immediate setting, to available resources, wider issues in the community and indeed to national policy. The tasks and aspects of practice being addressed will vary but for the EYP will also focus on quality delivery of EYFS provision. Team members will each approach the variety of tasks in distinctive ways and, clearly, human resource management is an important component of the role of leader of practice!

Bill is preparing for EYPS validation and currently works as the deputy manager of a workplace nursery, set up by the company for its personnel. Bill's role includes that of lead practitioner of the three- to five-year-olds but one Monday morning, he faces:

- *the manager phoning in to say she has broken her leg and will be off work for at least six weeks, so Bill would need to cover her role;*
- *concern from Maria, Bill's 'second' in the pre-school room about how she would cope with being the lead practitioner while Bill covered the manager's role;*
- *a phone call from a distressed parent of one of the babies expressing concern that after collecting her child the previous Friday, she had found a bruise on her baby's leg and there had been no reference to this either orally from the key person or in the Baby Diary which is used for two-way communication.*

Think of the person, environmental and task variables which Bill (and others in the staff team) face at the present time. What effect might these be having on team cohesion and effectiveness? What leadership skills will Bill need to apply in dealing with these current challenges?

Leadership of practice with a team

As we have stressed, the role of EYP is not to be confused with that of team leader, but we have identified that leadership of practice is usually carried out in a team context and in this section, we focus specifically on different aspects of the EYP role as leader within a team. Becoming an effective team requires the commitment and effort of every team member but in leading practice, particularly in effecting change, you may well have a crucial role in determining team cohesion.

The EYP should demonstrate principled leadership (Isaksen and Tidd, 2006; Rodd, 2006). We have already identified the importance of the value stance of the leader of practice, leading by example, encouraging and implementing new ideas and sharing best practices. The principled leader recognises that some in the team will need more support than others, requiring encouragement to express their own ideas confidently within the team. The model of leadership demonstrated by the EYP is not one that exerts authority over others but rather one that empowers each individual to maximise her/his distinctive contribution to the whole. This is collaborative leadership: Whalley (2005b) refers to such a dynamic as a 'leaderful team' where all are committed to 'growing learning communities'.

One of your key tasks as leader of practice, then, is to engage all relevant members of your team in identifying the challenges and opportunities for improvements in your setting and then sharing responsibility for transforming ideas into action. Pound (2005) refers to this as 'distributed leadership' and this is useful in enhancing our understanding of the EYP leadership role, especially in effecting change. You will need to demonstrate competence in taking a lead in collaborative decision-making.

Look at these examples from four EYPs, showing how they have evidenced S33–35.

Example 1 – Kate, proprietor and manager of a day nursery:

'I worked with each of the heads of room in the setting and together we modelled to the rest of the team how to note down daily observations of activities that the children had particularly enjoyed, particular achievements, etc. and then to reflect on how this learning might be extended. I then encouraged each team to use these observations to inform the following week's plans.'

Example 2 – Angela, advisory teacher for a group of private nurseries:

'Working across different settings has been particularly challenging but I spent a lot of time building up good relationships with individual managers and colleagues in our settings and aimed to model to them the importance of close teamwork, with each making their own personal contribution to the setting. Together we discussed the Ofsted inspection framework and how our practice should aim to incorporate the *Every Child Matters* outcomes into everyday practice. I produced a "Care, Learning and Inclusion" file for each setting and worked with staff on a monitoring sheet which is used to regularly appraise how this is going.'

Example 3 – Joanne, manager of a private nursery:

'I know I still have a lot to learn and am prepared to develop my skills continually. I believe communication is very positive in the nursery and my staff have a lot of respect for me and I value this. I know the staff appreciate the support I give them in the rooms and are always proud to share with me their ideas and achievements. I take time to listen to their ideas and tease them out so that decisions about changes to practice are shared.'

Example 4 – Lewis, co-supervisor in a pre-school:

'I was an accountant before I made a career change to Early Years practice and never considered myself to have "leadership skills". I really like the fact that Sonia (co-leader) and I share responsibilities here but even then we would rarely impose our ideas on the team. Instead, we review practice at our monthly team meetings and when we have a particular challenge or opportunity, such as the water-logged outdoor play area we have at present, we all brainstorm possible solutions and share action on these.'

REFLECTIVE TASK

- *How are Kate, Angela, Joanne and Lewis each demonstrating a collaborative leadership style?*

- *Can you begin to identify examples from your practice which demonstrate your own skill here and you might use as evidence as you prepare for EYP validation?*

Partnership with families

The concept of a 'triangle of care' – with a partnership between parents and professionals to best support the child – has been around since the 1994 Start Right Report (Ball, 1994). One of the key tasks of Early Years practitioners is to establish strong partnerships with parents as the child's 'first and most enduring educators' (DFEE, 2000). Since then, this has been identified as a core practice issue in a number of research reports (Bertram and Pascal, 2002; Siraj-Blatchford et al., 2002; Sylva et al., 2004). Indeed, we have already seen that the key person role is now a statutory requirement of the EYFS (DCSF 2008a) and the triangular relationship of key person, child and family is essential in nurturing children's emotional, cognitive and physical well-being.

Early Years practice in this country has been influenced by the pioneering work of the Reggio Emilia pre-schools in northern Italy, where the pedagogical approach places families at the heart of an alliance of practitioners, the community – including local artists – and policy makers (Thornton and Brunton, 2007). Equally, there are currently many strong examples of effective setting–parent partnerships in Early Years settings in the UK, such as the Thomas Coram Centre in London and the Pen Green Centre in Northamptonshire. The innovative partnership work developed by Margy Whalley and the team at Pen Green has proved to be particularly inspiring to many Early Years practitioners. Pen Green is set in a socially challenging area but, since the 1980s, staff have been committed to 'engaging parents as decision makers in the planning and implementation of work at the centre' (Whalley et al., 2007: 7) and over recent decades a collaborative culture has been established which seeks to value the decisions and choices of children, staff and parents. The outcomes for children and families at Pen Green have been remarkable and are a reminder of the 'great untapped energy and ability of parents and their deep commitment to supporting their children's development' (Whalley et al. 2007: 32).

REFLECTIVE TASK

Margy Whalley at Pen Green states that Early Years practitioners need to take time to establish 'equal, active and responsible partnerships with parents' (Whalley and Pen Green, 2007: 32).

- *Are you able to identify particular strengths in this area of your own practice?*

- *What specific opportunities and challenges do you face in leading others in understanding the importance of partnership with families?*

EYP Standards 29–32 focus specifically on working in partnership with families and carers. The ideal of parents playing a major role in their children's learning now passes virtually uncontested but the reality is often more challenging. Any involvement must be at the family's own pace and in the way in which they are most comfortable. EYPs need to be alert to both the potential of parental involvement and to the real pressures on families. Many working parents feel they have limited energy to 'support' their child's learning in the way that many of our Early Years settings would like. Equally, many are themselves facing domestic, social or financial challenges which sap energy.

A further challenge to parent partnership lies in differences in understanding of the purpose of Early Years provision. Many parents appear to succumb to the seductive pressure of marketing and purchase expensive (and arguably unnecessary) pre-school learning resources. Others actively challenge the emphasis on play-based learning embedded within the EYFS framework. Some settings can have a tendency to demand too much of parents, asking them almost to take on the role of 'teacher'. Karpf (2007) suggests that this trend might be seen to favour highly educated parents and thus actually widen, rather than narrow, the gap between families. Space does not allow wider discussion of these complex issues but what is important is that practitioners believe parents to be 'experts on the subject of their own children' (Whalley et al., 2007: 65) and are enabled and empowered to share this expertise with practitioners.

Look at the following accounts from EYPs which highlight different aspects of partnership with families.

CASE STUDY

Andrea, childminder

'Arthur, 2 years 2 months, was about to start in my home setting for three days a week while his mother, Helena, returned to work. I thought we had prepared well for this: I had visited their home, they had made a number of shared visits to mine. I had gathered a lot of key information from Helena and Arthur about him – his preferences, interests, routines, etc. Then on the day Helena dropped him off for the first time, she handed me his bag and said: "I've put his flash cards in there . . . he does them for 10 minutes in the morning and 10 minutes in the afternoon". This was so much against the pedagogical base for my own practice – yet I also wanted to work in partnership with the family!'

Theresa, Family Support Worker in a children's centre

'As part of my role, I work with Parbeen and her son, Mohan, who is 3 years 5 months and has recently been identified as on the autistic spectrum. Parbeen had admitted to the health visitor some months ago that she was finding it hard to manage Mohan's behaviour but has shown significant resistance to this diagnosis and has kept insisting there is "nothing wrong" with Mohan. I have tried to defuse her anxiety by stressing that we want to work together in Mohan's best interests. One way we are doing this is by sharing a diary – of notes and photographs, from home and setting – to document Mohan's achievements.'

Matt is room leader of a 15-place pre-school room (3–4-year-olds) in a private nursery.

Jemima is now 3 years 6 months old and most children by that age are ready to make the transition into the pre-school from the toddler room. However, despite using our usual system whereby the key person accompanies a toddler into the pre-school for short sessions over a period of weeks, Jemima is still tearful and anxious whenever she comes up to us. Tara, Jemima's mum, feels it is in Jemima's best interest to stay in the toddler room for the time being. The manager, Lenny (Jemima's key person) and myself met with Tara to discuss this and we have agreed to Tara's request and will review in six weeks' time.'

REFLECTIVE TASK

- *In what ways are Andrea, Theresa and Matt demonstrating skills in working with parents?*
- *In what ways are practitioner and parent working collaboratively here? In particular, what would you do if you were Andrea?*
- *What opportunities for leadership do these EYPs have here?*
- *Are you able to identify examples from your own practice of effective partnership with families?*

Managing conflict situations in partnership work

In order to lead practice effectively, the EYP requires social skills and emotional intelligence. This is true, equally, of collaborative working with colleagues and of partnership working with families. Much has been documented about 'emotional intelligence' (see, for example, Gardner, 1983; Goleman, 1996). Increasingly, emotional factors have become a recognised aspect of educational thinking and practice (Moyles, 2001). This focus was translated into policy when children's social and emotional well-being was highlighted as an essential concern for all organisations that work with children (DfES, 2004a). The emotional dimension is, therefore, currently pertinent to your role as an EYP. This awareness of emotional matters has been conceptualised as 'emotional literacy' (Bubb, 2005).

Such emotional intelligence is critical to managing difficulties that can arise within teams. Few people welcome conflict but a healthy and emotionally intelligent attitude recognises that it is an inevitable part of teamwork and, indeed, the process of conflict resolution can often result in a stronger team (Noone, 1996). Within the EYP role, you should recognise the importance of modelling an appropriate way to deal with conflict situations constructively and creatively,

Conflict can be caused by the following:

- mis- or incomplete information;
- resistance to change;

- pressure to conform – limiting individual preferences;

- 'group think' – where the group converges on a decision that seems to have greatest agreement regardless of quality;

- dominant individuals and the consequent inequality of influence on decisions and outcomes;

- inability to accept feedback or criticism;

- lack of individual accountability – 'the team takes ownership';

- interpersonal conflict – unproductive levels of competition leading to 'winners' and 'losers'.

(Based on Isaksen and Tidd, 2005)

In identifying and addressing any of these challenges to effective teamwork, the skilled EYP should employ conflict resolution strategies, including active listening; observing and noting any non-verbal clues; helping those involved to understand and define the problem; allowing feelings to be expressed; looking for alternative, workable solutions; and encouraging individuals involved to take responsibility to implement these solutions (Armstrong, 1994, cited in Rodd, 2006).

CASE STUDY

Vic, preparing for EYPS validation

Vic is room leader of the pre-school group in an independent nursery. He works very well with two other colleagues, Betty (who has worked in the nursery for 20 years) and Judith. When Judith begins her maternity leave, Tammy joins the team to cover for her. Tammy has only recently qualified as an Early Years practitioner and is confident and enthusiastic, with lots of ideas about how Early Years practice should be organised. Vic and Tammy establish a strong rapport but Vic soon begins to notice the change in Betty who becomes quite withdrawn, arrives at the last minute and leaves as soon as she can at the end of day, contributes little in team meetings, and generally appears to be losing her enthusiasm for her work. Vic realises this is having an impact on team morale and indirectly on the quality of provision for the children.

REFLECTIVE TASK

- *What do you think is happening in this scenario?*

- *What leadership skills will Vic need to manage this situation effectively?*

- *Can you identify similar scenarios from your own practice, and if so, what was your role in resolving these?*

Similarly, there might be times when, as an EYP, you need to deal with an angry, upset or anxious parent. Such situations provide you with opportunities to draw on your own skills and professional expertise and to empower parents in their own role. Such situations also allow you to demonstrate to colleagues a respectful and attentive approach to partnership work. One of the four themes of the EYFS is that of 'positive relationships' and you might think here of the specific opportunities you have as an EYP to demonstrate these in your work with parents:

- at key moments of transition: from home to setting, within the setting and to the next provider (Standard 3);

- involving parents in their children's learning, development and well-being (Standard 29);

- opportunities for two-way communication with parents and for building relationships (Standard 30);

- opportunities for two-way sharing of information about children's achievements and progress (Standard 32).

However, there are times when such 'opportunities' can result in conflict – though always with the possibility of a positive outcome! Consider the following case study and reflect on how Kate is drawing on her own knowledge and, at the same time, empowering the parents. The benefits to the child are huge in this case.

CASE STUDY

Kate, EYP and proprietor/manager of a private full-day care setting. Although she is super-numerary to staff ratios, Kate has a strong commitment to leading practice and giving a vision to the setting.

'We had a new child, Ezra (3 years 8 months) join our pre-school and, from the start, he was displaying some really unacceptable behaviours. It was crucial that Ezra's key person, Gloria, and myself meet with Ezra's parents as soon as possible. They kept putting off such a meeting and making excuses each time they came to collect him. After a few days, I intervened one afternoon and said it was really important that we meet and they reluctantly agreed to meet in my office the following morning. At first, there was little eye contact and some hostile remarks about this being a waste of time and so on. But as I outlined our concerns gently, describing Ezra in warm terms, the parents softened and eventually admitted that he was unruly at home, too, and they simply gave in to whatever he wanted to do. I encouraged Gloria to outline some key aspects of behaviour man-agement and, together, we formulated a strategy for both home and nursery: the adult would decide an appropriate response to a given situation and say to the child either "this is your choice" or "this is my choice". This approach allowed the child to retain many opportunities for his own choice but he had to begin to learn that sometimes he could not and to deal with the frustration of this. By the end of the meeting, it was clear that the parents too felt they were recovering some vestige of control in what was increasingly an out-of-control situation.'

REFLECTIVE TASK

- *How is Kate demonstrating her own skills in practice here and supporting Gloria in her practice?*

- *Can you think of similar examples from your own practice which are empowering parents?*

C H A P T E R   S U M M A R Y

Through reading this chapter, we hope you will feel clearer about the kind of evidence you might find to meet S29–32 and S33–36. In reflecting on the role of the EYP in leading practice within the context of 'partnerships', we have identified the importance of a principled and collaborative approach, based on respect, trust and high emotional intelligence. Theoretical aspects of team formation (Tuckman, 1965) and team roles (Belbin, 1993) have supported understanding of how teams work and insights from Pen Green have highlighted the importance of working in partnership with families. We have acknowledged that things can go wrong in partnership work when the EYP will need to demonstrate skills in managing conflict.

Moving on

In the next chapter we develop the concept of partnership working and reflect on the opportunities and challenges of working within a multi-professional context. In order to meet the complex needs of children and families, it is important that a wide range of professionals are involved and a spirit of collaboration and cooperation established between them. Thus, the EYP needs to develop the skills required to work with agencies external to the setting.

Self-assessment questions

Use this exercise to reflect on your learning from this chapter and to think further about your skills in leading practice within a team context.

1. Think again about Tuckman and Jensen's work on the five stages on team formation. Focus on the performing stage and think about how teams reach the point of 'optimum performance' (Answer: page 99). How does the EYP lead practice in such a way as to maximise the potential of each team member?

2. What is distinctive about Belbin's (1993) work on team roles and the defining of contributions that each role brings to a team (Answer: page 102)? What have you learned about the different roles played by colleagues in your setting's team?

3. What are the five 'S' factors that can affect group/team cohesion (Answer: page 103)? Think of your setting. Are these positive or negative factors in your team's setting? What can you do about any hindering factors?

4. What are the four principles outlined by Gillen (1995) for building and maintaining an effective team (Answer: page 100)? How far do you believe you put these into practice in your own role as leader of practice?

5. What are the three types of variable in any team identified by Burton and Dimbleby (1988) (Answer: page 105)? How do you ensure you take each of these into account when you lead practice?

6. Carry out a self-audit of skills in collaborative working with parents and families.

Aspect of practice	Personal strengths/ experience	Skills in/opportunities to lead practice and links with EYPS Standards	Issues for development
Partnership in children's learning and development			
Continuity and progression, including transitions			
Empowerment and educational opportunities for parents/families			
Modes of communication: • routine • written • oral • visual			

7. What are some of the possible causes of tension and conflict in a team (Answer: pages 110–111)? What skills does the EYP need in order to role-model healthy relationships and to help resolve conflict where it exists?

FURTHER READING

The Mind Tools website offers some useful guidance on working effectively within a team. In particular, look at the 'Leadership Skills' and 'Team management' in Explore the Tool Kit www.mindtools.com

Pen Green Team (2007) 'All About . . . working with parents'. Available on the EYFS CD-Rom: The Early Years Foundation Stage, file://D:/resources/downloads/2.2_a.pdf

8 Leading practice in a multi-professional context

CHAPTER OBJECTIVES

In this chapter we identify key factors in effective and successful partnership working with different professionals within a setting and with external agencies. There is discussion around engagement and involvement with these partners in Early Years practice. In focusing on the role of the leader of practice, we consider ways of supporting colleagues to work more effectively with other professionals. Work within multi-professional contexts can be complex; we will explore some issues surrounding this work and also consider opportunities for EYPs' leadership of practice through reflective tasks and self-assessment exercises which aim to support you in leading and enabling a collaborative approach to improving practice and developing collective accountability.

After reading this chapter you should be able to:
- reflect on the importance of collaboration with other professionals both within and beyond the Early Years setting;
- understand how to work collaboratively with other professionals;
- critically appraise your own strengths and areas for development in leading collaborative practice within a multi-professional context;
- apply your understanding to the preparation of your evidence for EYP validation.

S6 and S36 are particularly relevant to this chapter but you are encouraged to reflect broadly across other Standards as you seek to apply your knowledge, understanding and skills in partnership work with other professionals to all aspects of your practice.

Introduction

Early identification and provision of help is in the child's best interests and multiagency services which deliver support for families are vital in promoting children's well being . . . All who come into contact with families have a part to play in identifying those children whose needs are not being adequately met.

(Munro, 2011: 10–11)

Since the beginning of the twenty-first century we have seen an increasing movement towards integrated working with children and young people: a multi-professional, collaborative approach. The EYFS Framework identifies practitioners' work within multi-professional contexts as an integral part of their role; successful delivery of the EYFS is underpinned by partnership working with parents, other practitioners and with professionals from other agencies (DCSF, 2008a).

Effective collaboration within a team (S33–35) and partnership working with families (S29–32) were the focus of the last chapter but the EYP Standards also reflect an emphasis on integrated delivery. S36 is particularly relevant here as it explicitly relates to EYPs' work within multi-professional contexts, including the coordination and implementation of programmes and interventions, which have been agreed by the multi-professional team (CWDC, 2010a: 79). This work is underpinned by EYPs' secure knowledge and under-standing of the contribution that other professionals can make to children's emotional and physical well-being, learning and development (S6) (CWDC, 2010a: 23).

In this chapter, then, we extend the notion of partnership working to consider the importance of working collaboratively with other professionals to support the child and family more effectively. We focus on the EYP's role in developing and leading collaborative work within multi-professional contexts, which aims to improve outcomes for young children. While integrated service provision and formalised multi-professional working might not be part of the EYP role for some of you, it is important that you all understand how critical it is that you play your part, however small, in ensuring that everyone works together, each drawing on a specific bank of 'expertise', for the benefits of the children and their families.

Bronfenbrenner's ecological model

Our starting point is Bronfenbrenner's (1979) seminal ecological model of human develop-ment which offers a clear theoretical framework for our discussion on collaborative approaches to supporting young children and their families.

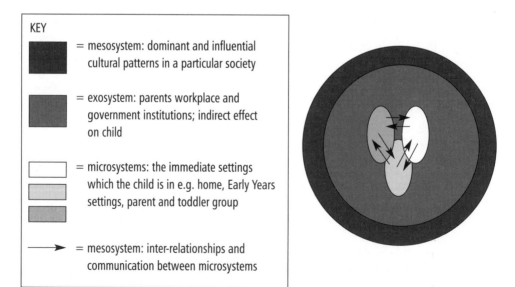

Figure 8.1 Bronfenbrenner's ecological model of human development

This model (see Figure 8.1), with the child at the centre, considers the different 'systems' to which the child is connected, each system influencing the other in a two-way state of reciprocal change (Garbarino and Abramowitz, 1992). The child is both influenced by and directly influences her/his environment. It can be argued that social policy is driven largely by the needs of families which, in turn, reflect the needs of individual children. The thrust of Bronfenbrenner's (1979) argument is that societies should place a high value on responding to the needs of young children but that this can only be achieved when 'members of that society acknowledge the complex interrelationship between children, parents, educators, carers, community groups and those responsible for key services' (Anning and Edwards, 2006: 3). It is the EYP's role to recognise and acknowledge these complex interrelationships and lead others in developing effective partnerships.

REFLECTIVE TASK

Begin to think about the various 'systems' to which a child belongs. Can you see how they interrelate? Think particularly about the connections between your setting and the child's home ('microsystems') and how you can encourage these.

Multi-professional contexts: policy development

The concept of collaborative working between professionals from different roles and children's services emerged at the end of the twentieth century. This was due to national policy initiatives that sought to improve outcomes for children; for instance, the introduction of the Sure Start Centres in disadvantaged communities, which aimed to reduce child poverty and social exclusion (Anning et al., 2006). These centres provided a multiagency approach to service delivery, which aimed to be more responsive to the local needs of families (Greenfield, 2011).

However, it was the Green Paper 'Every Child Matters (ECM): Change for Children' (DfES, 2003) and the ensuing 2004 Children Act that first advocated the necessity for improved collaborative working practices by all professionals involved in delivering children's services.

The outcomes of ECM are five wide-ranging objectives for children and young people, which were incorporated into the EYFS Framework. These outcomes are: Stay safe; Be healthy; Enjoy and achieve; Make a positive contribution; and Achieve economic well-being (DfES, 2004a).

The impetus to strengthen multi-agency approaches to service delivery was prompted by the conclusions of the Laming Report, following the tragic death of Victoria Climbié (Anning et al., 2006). Lord Laming (2003: 1) was critical of the 'buck passing' he had encountered from those who had sought to justify their position and called for 'clear lines of accountability'. The Laming report (2003: 4) found that the principal failure to protect Victoria Climbié from the fatal abuse to which she was subjected was the 'result of widespread organisational malaise'. The report, therefore, contained recommendations to ensure that departments worked more collaboratively and effectively together; for instance, it advised that each local authority should establish a 'Directorate of Children's

Services'. A joined-up approach to meeting the needs of families with young children had, therefore, become an imperative (Anning and Edwards, 2006).

An EYP describes her experience of working collaboratively and her understanding of the roles of other professionals and how she has used these to support parents and colleagues in her setting.

CASE STUDY

Carolynne, an EYP in a private nursery

'As an EYP in a children's centre, I am part of the process of collaborative work in the setting and have confidence to deal with other professionals. I explain to parents about the roles of other professionals who could be involved in working with their child – perhaps, when a professional wishes to meet with a parent or observe their child in the setting. My knowledge and experience about children's development helps me to explain how other professionals can support their child. I encourage parents to talk more openly, so I can have a better understanding of their perspective of collaborative working. I also support colleagues to deal with other professionals about a child in their care; for example, if they are meeting with them as the child's designated key person.'

PRACTICAL TASK

Now consider your own experience of working with other professionals and how you support others in the setting to work collaboratively. Look at Standard 6, which requires you to know the contribution that other professionals within and beyond the setting can make to children's physical and emotional well-being, development and learning (CWDC, 2010a: 23).

Consider your progress towards meeting these two aspects of S6 in the following task:

Aspect of S6	My current experience of this aspect of S6	Sources of evidence that could support my experience	Future action that could be required to meet this aspect of S6
I know and understand the roles of professionals who commonly support children from birth to the end of the EYFS			
I lead and support colleagues to develop their understanding of the contribution of, and ability to work collaboratively with other professionals within and beyond the setting			

Multi-professional contexts: implementation of policy

As an EYP, you might have involvement in writing and implementing policies concerning work in multi-professional contexts; these should be aimed at identifying and addressing children's needs and improving outcomes for them and their families and enabling children and families to access the full range of services that are available from different agencies, as required. Such policies are highly relevant to S36 and also link to S4–S6. Even if you are not directly involved in implementing such policies, you should still ensure that you are aware of the support that is available for young children and their families within the multi-professional contexts in which you work. This will enable you to assist them to access appropriate support and help other practitioners who work within multi-professional contexts to ensure children's outcomes are improved.

The Common Assessment Framework (CAF)

The Laming Report recommended the use of a National Assessment Framework and the Common Assessment Framework (CAF) is now the standardised approach to assessing children's additional needs. CAF aims to identify, at the earliest possible opportunity, any child's or young person's additional needs, not currently being met. As an EYP, you could be involved in contributing to a CAF or might support other practitioners within the CAF process, as well as supporting the child and their parents.

CAF is intended to promote partnership working to support individual families by using common procedures and protocols (Ball and Anning, 2008). There are four main stages in completing a common assessment: identifying needs early, assessing those needs, delivering integrated services and reviewing progress. The CAF assessment removes the need for different agencies concerned with providing services to undertake their own separate assessments and enables information to be accessible to all those involved in supporting the child's needs. National eCAF is the electronic application of CAF; this is a secure, web-based IT system designed for practitioners and managers who use CAF as part of their work with children.

CASE STUDY

Katie, an EYP in a children's centre

'I realised there was a lot of information on CAF in the setting but it came from different sources and was saved in different places. Therefore, I wanted to put all of the information into one central place that was easily accessible for all practitioners. I met with the Senior Family Support Worker about creating a folder and we shared ideas on this. I also met the CAF coordinator for the borough and collected useful information which could go into the CAF folder and did some internet research of my own. Since introducing the folder on CAF into the Children's Centre, I have seen it used by many professionals. It is accessible to everyone.'

REFLECTIVE TASK

Reflecting on Katie's account about developing her understanding about CAF and supporting others in her setting, consider:

- *how you ensure that you have the most up-to-date information on policy issues relating to multi-agency working;*

- *how you disseminate this information to colleagues and lead on its impact on practice in your setting.*

The lead professional

Any practitioner involved in working with the child and their family can contribute to the CAF process but there is a named lead professional who oversees the provision of agreed services, convenes multi-professional meetings and is the main point of contact for the family (Greenfield, 2011). By coordinating the delivery of actions agreed by practitioners involved in the multi-agency 'Team around the child' (TAC), the lead professional ensures that children and their families receive an effective, integrated service that is regularly reviewed. The TAC is established on a case-by-case basis to support the needs of child and family at the centre of the process. Once their consent has been gained to share information, one practitioner advises other professionals from relevant services to form a TAC. By coming together, the team can then review information collected from discussions, assess identified needs and decide on a suitable course of action to provide the required services. The designated lead professional coordinates the work of the TAC. The actions are based on the outcome of the CAF and are then recorded on the CAF delivery plan. By acting as a single point of contact, the lead professional can reduce stress for families who are being supported by a number of different agencies (Baldock et al., 2009).

Information sharing

Information sharing is the term used to describe the situation where practitioners use their professional judgement and experience on a case-by-case basis to decide whether and what personal information to share with other practitioners in order to meet the needs of a child. The Laming Report (2003) suggested that agencies should share information more effectively; and clear expectations for local action to improve information sharing are set out in the 2004 Children Act. Children's Trust Boards should ensure that all partners consistently apply the 'Information Sharing Guidance' so that:

- all practitioners are aware of, and have access to, the information-sharing guidance and training, and are confident in making decisions about information sharing;

- the organisational and cultural aspects that are required to embed information sharing have been, or are being, addressed.

(DCSF, 2010c: 44)

Safeguarding

All registered providers, with the exception of childminders, are required to have a designated practitioner to take lead responsibility for safeguarding children within the setting and liaise with local statutory children's services agencies as appropriate (DCSF, 2008a). The Laming Report used the term 'safeguarding' rather than 'child protection', when talking about children's welfare, to highlight that all professionals must share the responsibility to support the child's well-being (Anning and Hall, 2008). Professionals from different children's services, such as education, health, and social care are expected to provide coordinated support for individual children, particularly for those at the greatest risk of being harmed. The EYFS Framework provides clear guidance about safeguarding across three main aspects of practice:

- safeguarding and promoting children's welfare;

- promoting the children's good health; preventing the spread of infection and taking appropriate action when they are ill;

- effectively managing children's behaviour, in a manner that is appropriate for their stage of development and particular individual needs.

(Adapted from DCSF, 2008a: 19)

Depending on the nature of the safeguarding issue, Early Years practitioners engage in multi-professional contexts when dealing with aspects of safeguarding, using appropriate policies and procedures as required. Professionals engaged in safeguarding action are expected to embrace a 'culture of listening' (DCSF, 2010c: 42); seeking children's views, in age-appropriate ways, and taking their views into account when individual decisions are made or when services are established or developed (DCSF, 2010c).

Look at how these EYPs engaged with other professionals and sought children's views when developing different aspects of safeguarding in their setting.

CASE STUDY

Tracey, an EYP in a children's centre

'Following an inspiring course on "Safeguarding Children", I passed on information to other practitioners in the centre. We thought it would be useful to make posters with the children about safeguarding issues that would help people understand about safety in the setting. The children were keen to be involved and I arranged for a visit from the community police officer. We thought about different scenarios we could use for the posters and the best places where we should place them. The children enjoyed making these posters and they have raised awareness of safeguarding in the setting – the manager has since asked me to translate the Safeguarding Policy into one of the centre's community languages and we are now looking at other ways to ensure that the Safeguarding policy is understood by everyone using the centre.'

CASE STUDY

Maria, an EYP in a children's centre

'Safeguarding protects children from maltreatment and ensures that children grow up in circumstances consistent with the provision of safe and effective care. The children had access to a woodwork area so I promoted safeguarding in my setting by creating rules for use of this area, to ensure that it was a safe place for them to be. I sought advice from a teacher in a nearby school and then talked with the children about rules and why we might need them. They were very interested in the rules and we decided we would need a rule about wearing goggles at all times, making sure that there are two hands on a saw when cutting wood and only having two children cutting wood at any time. I then took photos of the children in the woodwork area, complying with the rules and we displayed them around the area so that they could be seen and remembered by everyone using the area.'

CASE STUDY

Elena, an EYP in a children's centre

'The children were very interested in the story of "Handa's Surprise" (Browne, 1995); I realised that we could look at the importance of being healthy by using this story, which they liked so much. I shared this with the staff and we planned to involve other professionals to talk about health. I carried out a risk assessment to make sure that all resources were safe to use and checked if any children had food allergies. Referring to the story, we then made fruit kebabs; the children were keen to cut and taste the fruit, even though they had not tasted some items previously. By asking open-ended questions, I enabled the children to express how they felt about the experience. We then developed displays and role-play activities from the story. I liaised with the local lead practitioner for Oral Health Promotion, who came to talk with the children on how to keep their teeth clean and healthy. Other practitioners observed their key children in the sessions. Their feedback was positive as they, too, had enjoyed the visit. I posted details about the session in the parents' newsletter and received positive feedback from them about their children's interest in brushing their teeth at home. As an EYP, it is my responsibility to make sure that the children have knowledge about how to be healthy. Talking about healthy foods and being active will help the children become more confident to try new things and explore the world around them.'

CASE STUDY

Laura, an EYP working as a childminder in her own home

'When new children start in my setting, I spend a lot of time sharing my policies and procedures with parents. I feel it's really important that I explain to them the importance I

place on safeguarding the children and, with their children, I show them round my home and garden – pointing out the safety procedures I have in place which I consider part of the "quality practice" I seek to offer. I recently had a new two-year-old start who has impaired mobility and I was a little concerned about the safety of my outdoor area. Through the local Childminders' Network, I was put in touch with an advisory teacher who joined us for the preliminary visit and helped me to carry out a risk assessment through observing the child in the garden. It was important to look at the garden through the child's "eyes" and also to listen to the views of her parents.'

Reflecting on these accounts, consider how Tracey, Maria, Elena and Laura:

- *model 'a culture of listening' in their setting; they recognise that children's views should be sought and their views taken into account (as appropriate), when developing shared knowledge and understanding about aspects of Safeguarding (DCSF, 2010c);*

- *appreciate that different forms of communication can be used when working collaboratively to help share knowledge and understanding of policy;*

- *understand that a safe environment is one 'where safety is not seen as safety from all possible harm but offers safety to explore, experiment, try things out and take risks' (Tovey, 2007: 102);*

- *use children's ideas and interests when starting conversations; this helps adult interactions to be based in a responsive approach and supports the development and enrichment of children's knowledge, skills and understanding.*

(Broadhead et al., 2010)

Multi-professional working: *Common Core of Skills and Knowledge*

Safeguarding is one of the six areas of expertise in the 'Common Core of Skills and Knowledge' (CWDC, 2010c), which describes the skills and knowledge that are expected of those who work with children and young people. The six areas, which were revised in 2010, underpin multi-agency and integrated working, professional standards, training and qualifications across the children and young people's workforce. They are:

- effective communication and engagement with children, young people and families;

- child and young person development;

- safeguarding and promoting the welfare of the child or young person;

- supporting transitions;

- multi-agency and integrated working;

- information sharing.

(Adapted from CWDC, 2010c: 2)

Multi-professional working: *One Children's Workforce Framework*

The 'One Children's Workforce Framework' is a representation of an integrated workforce (CWDC, 2010d). It aims to help everyone to work together more effectively to improve outcomes for children and young people. Each strand has a designated colour of the rainbow, in much the same way that the EYFS uses different colours to present its four themes. The areas of the one children's framework and their corresponding colours are:

- shared identity, purpose and vision (red);

- common values and language (orange);

- behaviours focused on positive outcomes for children and young people (yellow);

- integrated working practices (green);

- high-quality, appropriately trained workforce (blue);

- complementary roles focused around children and young people (indigo);

- capacity to deliver and keep children safe (violet).

(Adapted from CWDC, 2010d)

An effective model of multi-professional working was reported by Bertram et al. (2002: 10) in their evaluation of the Early Excellence Centre (EEC) Pilot Programme. The evaluation found that integrated services offered a 'multi-professional and multi-faceted response' that was crafted around an individual family. This provided service users with a flexible and effective response. The report identified three core characteristics of the EEC integrated services; they demonstrated:

1. a specialised, coordinated and planned application to a professionally identified need;

2. an individualised nature that was shaped in response to the particular needs of a family or individual;

3. a non-judgemental, respectful and empowering character that acknowledged cultural and social diversity, and encouraging agency and responsibility within the family.

(Adapted from Bertram et al., 2002: 10)

Think about different aspects of your own practice, particularly those which involve working with other professionals.

- *How would you characterise the response provided at your setting?*

- *Are you able to trace any 'improvements' in the delivery of services that you support which are resulting in better outcomes for children and families? (S36)*

- *How do you ensure that colleagues understand their role as part of a multi-professional team and can make an appropriate contribution? (S36)*

Make a note of your reflections.

Collaborative practice within multi-professional contexts

The review has been impressed by those local innovations that have tackled this problem by creating multi agency teams where concerns can be examined and more accurate judgements made about what level and type of help is needed. Common to these successes has been the creation of channels through which practitioners from different agencies can discuss their concerns, either in a meeting room or simply over the telephone. The value of these informal but strategic conversations is that they enable professionals to exchange ideas without needing to enter formal proceedings.

(Munro, 2011: 32–33)

EYPs' collaborative work within multi-professional teams requires the provision of 'succinct, timely and evidence-based information, provided with the full knowledge of parents' (S36) (CWDC, 2010a: 79). Powell (2007: 24) suggests that failure in inter-agency collaboration and communication can occur partly because of a 'lack of desire' to relinquish specific involvement and to accept the need for other professional intervention. Perhaps in the past this has been the case and there remains a residue of such an attitude, but increasingly professionals are recognising that they each have an equal but distinctively different role to play in effective service provision for children and their families. As an EYP you can be confident of the distinctive professional contribution you make through your expertise in specialist knowledge of the principles and content of the EYFS and of child development (Standards 1 and 2). Nonetheless there are challenges here (Anning et al., 2006; Powell, 2007) and potential barriers to effective inter-professional communication and collaboration. These include:

- confusion about parameters of roles and responsibilities – especially in working together while acknowledging the importance of specialist expertise;

- disappointment and frustration about slowness or lack of change;

- conflicting priorities and work practices;

- little systematic or effective sharing;
- exclusion of others by the use of jargon.

However, the findings, cited above in Professor Munro's report (2011), provide an encouraging perspective on how channels of communication can be established, which facilitate the development of shared understandings; this enables services to be appropriately matched and targeted at those in most need. EYPs should support all individuals involved in collaborative working, who, in turn, are expected to demonstrate mutual respect for the expertise of others to support the shared aims of the agencies involved in working with the child and their family (CWDC, 2010c).

Consider ways in which collaboration and communication were fostered in the following account, which describes how an EYP promoted safeguarding in her setting and worked with others to improve safeguarding procedures.

CASE STUDY

Adepeju, an EYP in a Children's Centre

'On a few occasions, I had witnessed the gate and entrance door to the centre being left open which posed a real threat to the safety of the children, as well as parents and staff in the building. Leaving gates or doors open could lead to unauthorised entry into the building which could put children at risk – and situations like this can be avoided. I discussed the issue with the manager and staff and they agreed something needed to be done, so I put up a new sign in order to alert people of the danger.

Though only simple, the safety sign on the gate and door in question has been effective as it fulfils the requirement to safeguard children against intruders. It also serves as a reminder for parents, members of staff and visitors of the importance of ensuring that the gate and door are closed properly when coming in and leaving the premises and conveys the message of team working in order to safeguard children – parents and centre workers need to work together to ensure children's safety.

A week later, I led a discussion with practitioners on "who are you letting into the setting", which provided a forum for reflection on safeguarding children. This experience thus supported other practitioners to reflect on their individual practice in regards to safeguarding children and themselves. It was interesting to see how a gently persuasive message can make a great impact on people's attitudes by sharing responsibilities.'

REFLECTIVE TASK

Reflecting on this case study, consider how Adepeju supported knowledge and understanding about safeguarding in the setting. In what ways did Adepeju:

- *demonstrate personal accountability;*
- *encourage awareness of safeguarding issues;*

- *create a 'no blame' culture;*

- *demonstrate leadership;*

- *develop collaborative approaches to safeguarding;*

- *support other practitioners to reflect on their own practice;*

- *keep the child at the centre?*

PRACTICAL TASK

Now consider how you could promote knowledge and understanding of an aspect of collaborative practice in collaboration with others. How would you draw upon their expertise and experience to make the message effective? An example is given in the table below:

Proposed aspect of collaborative practice	People involved	Relevant EYP Standards
Developing the natural environment in the outdoor area of the setting	Children, Parents, Staff; Local garden centre manager; LA EY Advisor; Children's Centre outreach worker	S1, S5, S6, S8, S11, S12, S18, S19, S20, S24, S29, S31, S33–39

In their 2007 study, *Effective Leadership in the Early Years (ELEYS)*, Siraj-Blatchford and Manni identify a commitment to collaboration as one of the fundamental requirements for the leadership role in early childhood. Clearly, as an EYP, you will seek to effectively contribute to the work of multi-professional teams but might not be the most appropriate person in the setting, for example, to join the TAC. Therefore, you would need to evaluate if it was appropriate for you to participate in a multi-professional context. You should also consider training opportunities, that might support you to contribute more effectively within multi-professional working, as well as supporting others to take up professional development opportunities, as necessary (S38). In the report on Early Intervention, Allen (2010: 56) describes Children's Centres' successful implementation of 'user-friendly and integrated services that reach disadvantaged communities'; however, he also warns us about the need for continued workforce development to support effective provision which 'matters to child outcomes'.

All practitioners have a responsibility to work collaboratively within multi-professional contexts, regardless of their role within the setting (Ford, 2009). When everyone shares the responsibility for the child, however, it might be unclear who is responsible at any particular time (Luckock, 2010). Clear communication is, therefore, essential to ensuring that the work of the multi-professional team is on course to provide the required support and that everyone concerned is informed of the progress towards the agreed outcomes. In the following case study, look at how Amir used clear communication and worked collaboratively with others to provide effective support for a child in his setting.

CASE STUDY

Amir, an EYP in a children's centre

'Before starting to work with Lucy, a 30-month-old girl with Down's Syndrome, I met with the nursery's Special Educational Needs Coordinator (SENCO). We discussed Lucy's development and needs and I obtained a copy of her Individual Educational Plan (IEP). I studied Lucy's details, observed her and met with her parents. I also read materials from professional organisations, which support children and adults with Down's Syndrome and viewed their videotapes. These helped me to familiarise myself with Down's Syndrome and provided information about reading and language. From my research, I was aware that Lucy was a visual learner and would benefit from support to accelerate her speech and language development, as this would assist her overall cognitive development.

My next step was to liaise with a speech and language therapist (SLT), who recommended the use of Makaton, a communication technique that uses speech, facial expression, gestures, signs and symbols to convey information. It is used to support language development, without replacing language. She demonstrated signing several rhymes using Makaton and I started implementing Makaton with Lucy immediately. I kept other practitioners in the nursery thoroughly informed of this initiative and its progress and, by displaying the signs on a wall chart and encouraging their use, both practitioners and other children started to use Makaton when communicating with Lucy.

Following the SLT's guidance, I designed a personalised signing dictionary for Lucy and created several rhyme sacks. These contained the key objects of reference for each rhyme (for example, a toy bus for "The Wheels On the Bus Go Round and Round") and I attached the rhyme sheet with Makaton's signs at the back of the sack. These sacks were used during Lucy's circle time with other children to expand her vocabulary. They reinforce her existing key vocabulary and help to introduce new concepts based on ones with which she is familiar. Pictures, signs and other visual cues used in this way utilise her strength as a visual learner. The rhyme sheet helps the continuity of the project, as practitioners refer to it when demonstrating the sign while Lucy takes the object out of its sack.

I kept Lucy's parents informed about the sacks and asked them if they would like to take them home. They were enthusiastic and supportive about using the sacks with Lucy. The marked progress in Lucy's sign usage and comprehension, her increased enthusiasm for participating in activities, as well as the opportunity to strengthen my relationship with her parents have all been immensely rewarding.

I believe that the high expectations of everyone in an Early Years setting need to be underpinned by the principle of inclusion. By liaising with other professionals and agencies and benefitting from their specialised insight and knowledge of Down's Syndrome, I have been able to provide support for Lucy and her family and ensure that colleagues can also understand and contribute to Lucy's provision, which is supporting her individual needs.'

REFLECTIVE TASK

Reflecting on this example of an EYP's collaborative work with others to support a child's individual needs, consider how Amir:

- *involved others in developing Lucy's provision;*

- *ensured that there was consistency of provision in the setting and at home;*

- *evaluated the impact of the provision;*

- *demonstrated leadership and support of others;*

- *took responsibility for professional development in order to make suitable provision.*

PRACTICAL TASK

This task aims to prompt your thinking about contributing and collaborating within multi-professional contexts. Look at the table below, which includes characteristics of multi-professional practice, and then add your response to the question. You might wish to complete this task with your mentor or a colleague.

Characteristics of effective participation within multi-professional teams

Characteristic	How do I demonstrate this characteristic?	Relevant EYP Standard
Be enthusiastic and committed		
See the 'greater good', regardless of short-term disadvantages		
Contribute sound professional knowledge		
Be willing to take on new challenges		
Engage and gain the understanding of others		
Be flexible and creative		

(Adapted from National College and Children's Workforce Network, 2009: 14)

C H A P T E R   S U M M A R Y

In this chapter, you have had the opportunity to reflect on how the EYP works collaboratively within a multi-professional context. First, we considered Bronfenbrenner's ecological model of human development, which provides a theoretical framework for the subject of multi-agency working. We then examined the background policy context to multi-agency working, which helps to explain its significance within current Early Years practice. Some of the challenges of working within multi-professional teams have been highlighted but we have also acknowledged benefits relating to inter-agency communication and collaboration. While integrated service provision and formalised multi-professional working might not be part of the EYP role for all of you, it is important that you each recognise the skills you need to contribute your professional expertise within a multi-professional context in order to support improved outcomes for all children and their families.

Moving on

In the next and final chapter, we focus on the final EYP Standards (S38 and S39). We acknowledge the importance of the EYP role in demonstrating an active commitment to continuing professional development and to inspiring and leading colleagues to take responsibility for identifying and meeting their own professional development needs. The core theme will be that of a 'community of learners' committed to a process of life-long learning, aspiring not only to establishing quality practice and provision but to continual reflection on and enhancement of their role. There are some current uncertainties about how the role of EYP will inhabit the Early Years workforce but you can draw on your resilience and 'repertoire of strategies' (CWDC, 2010a: 7) to embrace future challenge and continue to develop your professional role.

FURTHER READING

The CWDC website has helpful information to enhance your understanding of multi-professional work at: http://www.cwdcouncil.org.uk/integrated-working

Greenfield, S. (2011) Working in multidisciplinary teams. In Miller, L. and Cable, C. (eds) *Professionalization, Leadership and Management in the Early Years.* London: Sage.

9 Continuing professional development

CHAPTER OBJECTIVES

This final chapter offers the opportunity to define 'professionalism' as core to the EYP role and its application in the context of contemporary Early Years practice. We consider the importance of continuing professional development (CPD) for the EYP, especially in refining and redefining understanding of 'leadership' of practice. We discuss how CPD is crucial to building and sustaining self-confidence in this role, particularly in nurturing the confidence and competence of others. The creation and maintenance of a constructive approach to self-evaluation within Early Years settings is outlined and the role of the EYP in leading and supporting others in self-critical practice is addressed. One important aspect of the EYP role lies in identifying and encouraging the EYPs of the future. Case studies and reflective tasks are offered to support these themes.

After reading this chapter you should be able to:
- understand the concept of 'professionalism' within contemporary Early Years practice;
- identify the importance of continuing professional development for the leader of practice;
- evaluate the EYP role in supporting the continuing professional development of colleagues;
- appraise critically your own strengths and areas for development in these areas;
- apply your understanding to the preparation of your evidence for EYP validation.

This chapter has a broad focus and can be applied to all the EYP Standards as you seek to apply your knowledge, understanding to all aspects of your practice. You might like to focus on Standards 1–6 and on Standards 38 and 39 in particular.

Introduction

The concept of a 'profession' is commonly of a group of people who work in a 'defined way' and for an 'explicit purpose' (Nurse, 2007: 2). In the last chapter, there was much reference to inter-*professional* collaboration and multi-*professional* working, and by this it was clear we were referring to different spheres of employment: health; social work; family support; law enforcement and – for ourselves – Early Years practice. Here we pause to consider what we mean by professionalism in the context of Early Years practice. The emergence of the status of Early Years Professional, by its very name and validation process, is indicative of a drive to introduce a new understanding of professionalism into Early Years practice (Brock, 2006).

What, then, do we mean by the professional dimension to the EYP role? A positive and creative attitude to continuing professional development and lifelong learning is a key feature of this. As a leader of practice, you also have the responsibility of demonstrating this to colleagues and encouraging each of them to map and evidence their own professional development.

The professional role

How might we describe professional identity? Anning et al. (2006: 7) suggest that it is forged by 'a particular knowledge base, set of values, training and standing in the community'. What does this have to say about the dimensions of your professional role as an EYP? The 'knowledge base' is wide-ranging but refers particularly to your skills and expertise in leading the EYFS; and the awareness of and implications for practice of your own personal 'value stance'. The issue of your 'standing in the community' is much more complex. We have identified the historical legacy of a low-paid, predominantly female Early Years workforce which lacked a clearly defined career structure. Changes in public perception of the new professionalism within Early Years practice will not be swift and may take up to a generation to become rooted in public consciousness. Since the introduction of EYPS into the children's workforce, there has been growing debate about some of the issues relating to the increased professionalism which is implicit in this graduate role. There are many positive examples of the overall impact of the EYP role on the quality of provision for young children and, indeed, on the way it is leading to a greater sense of empowerment for many EYPs (CeDARE, 2011). Many practitioners now feel that their work and achievements are, at last, receiving the official recognition that their role deserves. Look at how one EYP describes this:

> *I have been able to build a new team, plan and organise the learning environment, work very closely with parents and – most importantly for me – lead on planning a child-led approach to provision for the children. This for me is the essence of my pedagogy as an EYP and I am delighted that Early Years practice is now viewed as a profession and that my achievements are being recognised.*
>
> (Claire, quoted in Whalley, 2011)

However, at the time of writing there remain many challenges and uncertainties in the way EYP Status is being embedded into the workforce. In particular, questions are rightly being asked about the gulf between the rhetoric of a 'world class transformational Early Years

sector with a highly qualified, fairly paid workforce' (Cooke and Lawton, 2008: 7) and the reality for many EYPs. Nevertheless, generally within the Early Years sector there is neither despair nor complacency. Indeed, the positive rigour required in the face of contemporary challenges might be said to define the professional approach required for the EYP role.

As you begin to explore how you are demonstrating the 'professionalism' within the EYP role, it might be helpful to think of this as a 'ball of knotted string' (Friedland, 2007: 126).

Friedland describes the particular 'knots' which need untying in order to untangle the ball and reach a clear definition. We have already touched on some of these but you might like to reflect again on their particular impact on your professional role: gender; the changing role of women in society; power and status; definitions of 'professionalism' in wider society; ethical dimensions; issues of leadership; policy drivers – nationally and locally; and pay structures.

Moyles (2001) offers further insights in defining professionalism in the Early Years, discussing this in the context of two further dimensions which she cites as 'passion' and 'paradox'. Moyles' main argument is for 'Early Years' to be viewed as a serious academic discipline and respected professional career pathway in its own right. Some years on, we might feel not only that was she right but that this has become well embedded within academia. The introduction of the DfES Sure Start Sector Endorsed Foundation Degree Early Years in 2002 and the EYP role in 2006 offers encouraging evidence for this. From research in both the UK and internationally, Moyles (2001) found that many Early Years practitioners expressed a passionate, highly enthusiastic commitment to their task. However, it is this passion, coupled with the particular challenges of the sector (the 'paradoxes') which is perceived as compromising the rigour by which early educators approach their work and, thus, the professional integrity of the role. Moyles argues that this is not the case and affirms strongly the distinctive element of passion, concluding:

> *Passion for young children is part of the culture of practitioners. Passion must be allowed, both as a panacea for coping with challenging paradoxes and also for inspiring professionalism in those who work and play with the youngest members of our society.*
>
> (Moyles, 2001: 93)

Look at the following case study where Leila, an EYP, describes her passion for her work, then reflect on the questions set to support your thinking about 'passion' and 'professionalism'.

CASE STUDY

Leila, a room leader in a Children's Centre

'I am absolutely passionate about what I do. I can't think of a better job! But I also know I have an awesome responsibility in helping shape the early learning experiences of young children and of engaging in partnership with their families in this. It's also not just about me; it's about a team approach here. There are days when things go wrong; the children's behaviour is very challenging, parents complain, there are difficulties within the staff team and then there are action plans to implement. I think if I lost the enthusiasm for the role I couldn't do it.'

- *What links can you draw between 'passion' and 'professionalism' here?*

- *How does this impact on the EYP role, especially in role-modelling good practice? Think about what motivates you in your role and how you are demonstrating professionalism in it.*

Rodd (2006) describes one of the products of becoming professional as additional moral/ethical obligations and responsibilities to children, their families, colleagues, the community and the wider profession itself. In the UK there is no formalised code of ethics for Early Years practice such as that developed in Australia (Australian Early Childhood Association Inc., 1991). While those with professional roles in Early Years settings might have a strong commitment to acting in the best interests of the children in their care, such a code of ethics would offer a 'valuable tool for guiding the complex decision-making faced in day to day work with young children and their families' (Rodd, 2006: 254). Your role as an EYP involves being reactive as well as proactive so, in addition to your role in planning and implementing change over time, you need to respond 'in the now' to situations that transpire and present themselves for immediate action. Many would agree that an accepted code of ethics for such times would create greater professional confidence.

Look at the range of issues facing Tamara on just one day in her practice and reflect on how she applies professionalism to the way she reacts to these.

Tamara, EYP and room leader of 3–4-year-olds in a full-day care setting, outlines some of the challenges she faced on one particular day

'One of my colleagues phoned me at 7 a.m. to let me know she would be off work because her daughter was poorly. She had also informed the manager so I hoped that there would be a "bank" Early Years practitioner coming in. When I arrived at work at 7.30, I learned that a prospective family was coming in that morning to look round the setting with a view to placing their 3-year-old son here and the bank staff, willing and competent as she was, had not worked at our setting before and so needed support to find her way round. As the children came in, one or two were upset to learn that my colleague was absent and rather diffident with the "bank" practitioner. The morning eventually went ok but, as I was beginning to think it was all right to take some non-contact time in the afternoon to complete some of the children's files, two of the boys in the room (both in my key group) began to develop some really interesting role play, developing from a pirate story they both loved.'

REFLECTIVE TASK

- *What are Tamara's professional choices here?*

- *What will guide her in decision-making?*

- *How might an agreed code of ethics support her in this?*

- *What would you do and why within this scenario?*

Anning and Edwards (2006: 51) describe professional identity in the EYP role as 'a way of being, seeing and responding', responsively and flexibly maximising the learning potential of every aspect of Early Years practice, particularly in building on the children's own ideas, preferences and interests (Carr, 2001). Your understanding of your own professionalism is a critical factor in determining how effectively you carry out the EYP role.

Continuing professional development

Pivotal to maintaining a professional stance is your commitment to ongoing professional development. Nutbrown (1996) described the right of every child to a 'respectful educator'. If we are to maintain the professional stance outlined above, you have a responsibility to be the best you can be in all aspects of the EYP role. Recommendations for improving practice and supporting professional development are clearly embedded in *the Early Years Foundation Stage* (DCFS, 2008b). EYP S33 stresses the important link between reflection and professional development; the more skilled you become in evaluating the effectiveness of your own practice, the more you will be able to identify opportunities to enhance and develop your own expertise and knowledge.

Anning and Edwards suggest that 'children learn to love learning through being with adults who also love to learn'. Indeed, they believe that the process of professional development for Early Years practitioners itself mirrors the early learning process. For children and educators alike, the dispositions for learning are of equal if not greater importance than the 'what?' and the 'how?' of learning. They describe the essential dispositions for the inquiring professional as developing:

- the capacity to see the educational potential in experiences shared with children;

- the capacity to respond to the demands they have identified as they work with children;

- dispositions for enquiry and learning;

- ways of seeing and being seen which draw on the professional expertise of Early Years practitioners.

(Anning and Edwards, 2006: 145)

These can be developed through reading, working with a critical friend, the professional appraisal process, attendance at in-service training (INSET) events, further accredited study and career development. Effective leadership requires commitment to both the 'acquisition and the dissemination of knowledge' (Waniginayake, 2006: xii).

REFLECTIVE TASK

Read the account by EYP Angela of her personal learning journey in Appendix one, and then consider the following questions.

- *How is Angela demonstrating her commitment to ongoing professional development?*

- *What does Angela's story tell you about the professional values she holds?*

- *Can you begin to map your own learning journey towards EYPS and clarify your own personal value stance towards your role?*

Much available literature focuses significantly on the role of the Early Years practitioner in action research (Abbott and Moylett, 1997; Anning and Edwards, 2006; Rodd, 2006; Bottle, 2007) and this is increasingly seen as a key component in professionalism and professional development. Rodd (2006: 213) describes this as a 'tool for narrowing the gap between research and practice that enhances professional learning and fosters reflective practice'. Indeed, strong links have been drawn between action research and quality improvement in the services provided for young children (Macnaughton et al., cited in Rodd, 2006). How, then, does action research sit with the EYP role?

Early Years practitioners in this country are not as confident about action research as their counterparts in other countries, where this aspect of practice is well embedded within the pedagogue role (Bottle, 2007). We have highlighted frequently that one of your tasks as an EYP is to make professional judgements about the children in your setting. Sound professional judgements are based to a large extent on the systematic collection and recording of information and the thoughtful analysis of this information based on wider reading (Willan, 2004).

Much of the inherited knowledge and many of the traditional practices within Early Years are based on research evidence from theorists such as Piaget, Vygotsky, Bruner, etc. You can read more about these in the child development literature such as Bee and Boyd (2006). Equally, few Early Years practitioners can be unaware of the international dimension of Early Years and how this, too, is influencing current practice, particularly the understanding of pedagogy emerging from Reggio Emilia (Abbott and Nutbrown, 2001) and the shape of the early childhood curriculum in New Zealand (New Zealand Ministry of Education, 1996). The influence and impact on contemporary Early Years provision of the early pioneers and major theorists and insights from other parts of the world cannot be overemphasised. However, as reflective EYPs, it is important to understand that no theory or framework can be imported 'whole' and imposed on a particular setting. We have clearly established the situational/contextual element of the EYP role and it is essential that you develop professional confidence in your own capacity to make judgements about the children and families in your setting, based on your own gathered evidence and wider reading.

Responsibilities for the professional development of colleagues

When asked how they encouraged the professional development of others, a group of EYPs offered the following.

> *I make sure I access relevant information in journals and on websites and then update and train staff on developments in Early Years.*
>
> (Manager, private day nursery)

> *I am currently implementing a programme of supervision of staff within the setting which also feeds directly into the individual training programme of the staff.*
>
> (Teacher, children's centre)

> *I encourage others within my network to attend training courses (and remind them when necessary). I buy and then lend books to colleagues which might be useful. For instance, I have found some excellent resources available on early communication and support for language development and I have been recommending these within the network.*
>
> (Childminder)

> *With my support, all the nurseries within our chain completed a quality accreditation scheme.*
>
> (Teacher, chain of private day nurseries)

In your lead role in effecting change (CWDC, 2010a) you will mainly be working alongside colleagues. The task of supporting others in their professional development is varied and will indeed include many of the elements identified above. You have a clear role in updating and training on developments in Early Years practice, particularly relating to the delivery of the EYFS. You will support quality enhancement in the setting and recommend training events and reading materials to colleagues. Within your role as mentor, you may well have key responsibilities in practitioner appraisal processes.

REFLECTIVE TASK

Take a few moments now to think about your role in supporting the professional development of colleagues. Can you describe how you see this in one or two sentences – as the EYPs quoted above have done? Note down your answer. In what way do you feel you are demonstrating leadership of practice in this role?

Consider here how a manager in a day nursery responded to this task:

I recognise the importance of my own professional development especially when I am tired and enthusiasm for the role is flagging. Engaging in professional development for myself gives me a push and I know that it can only strengthen me as a professional and that I can then pass on my skills to others.

(Manager, full-day care nursery)

In attending vigilantly to your own professional development and life-long learning journey you are transmitting powerful messages to colleagues and role-modelling effective practice. In your role as mentor to colleagues – which is integral to their professional development – you are engaging in *guided participation* (Rogoff, 1991). This is comparable to the child's experience of early learning in a safe and well-supported environment. One of your tasks in supporting the professional development of others is to empower and enable them to take their own learning forward by offering them a secure base from which to launch their professional development. You will best achieve this by actively encouraging them and listening to them as part of your role.

Drawing on their own research into professional development in the Early Years, Anning and Edwards (2006) conclude that guided participation is a critical factor. This is akin to the mentoring role where a more experienced practitioner supports a less experienced colleague by role-modelling appropriate actions and strategies. It also involves leading collaborative discussions on planning and reviewing change. You might support colleagues through joint collection and analysis of data, including sharing in any frameworks for data collection such as observation schedules. This will offer them a shared focus on the children's experience of learning and provision.

It was Dewey (1938) who first coined the concept of 'co-creating learning' in the school context. Rogoff (1991) developed this further, and the pedagogical principles of Reggio Emilia (Abbott and Nutbrown, 2001) and the work from the Pen Green Centre (Whalley, 2005b) root this firmly within the context of Early Years. Concepts such as 'communities of learners', with children, families and practitioners all 'co-creators in the learning process', will inspire you in the EYP role; you are encouraged to read more about the Pen Green

Centre and the work of the Reggio Emilia pre-schools and, if you have the opportunity, to visit them as part of your own continuing professional development.

You have a key role in leading practice by contributing to such an ethos of 'community learning' in your own setting. Louis et al. (1996, cited in Anning and Edwards, 2006) identify five significant components for an effective learning community. We have touched on a number of these already but they are included again here as they offer you a further opportunity to reflect on these aspects of practice and how you integrate these into your EYP role:

- **a shared sense of purpose** – bearing in mind that this takes time to achieve;

- **a collective focus on children's learning** – the creation of contexts, plans and evaluative actions taken to support children's holistic development;

- **purposeful collaborative activity** – this includes not only the immediate team of practitioner in the setting but also parents, families and other professionals involved with the practice in the setting;

- **deprivatised activity** – all practices need to be visible and transparent to colleagues and parents (Reggio Emilia settings use the documentation of children's learning as a key tool in deprivatising [Edwards and Forman, 1993]);

- **reflective dialogue** – leading evaluative discussion of key aspects of practice but also actively encouraging the full participation of colleagues.

REFLECTIVE TASK

For this task, read the account of Pia, who has developed a shared approach to professional development in her own setting, in Appendix 2.

- *Can you identify ways in which Pia has helped create a 'community of learners' in her own setting? How has she included all the 'stakeholders' here?*

- *Think about the three key factors that Pia identifies. How critical do you feel these to be in creating such a learning community?*

- *Are you able to identify more effective ways of encouraging the professional development of colleagues in your own setting?*

Identifying and encouraging future EYPs

In the EYP role, you are promoting autonomy within colleagues, encouraging them to identify their own professional development needs through a process of self-evaluation. The principles of reflective practice can be applied here as you role-model a self-evaluative/ appraisal approach to your own role and encourage colleagues to do the same. This will involve more than simply highlighting current strengths, areas for development in practice and any training needs; if effective, the process will also help colleagues to become more aware of their own value stance and to identify possible career plans.

- *Are you able to identify ways in which you support colleagues in effective self-evaluation or appraisal?*

- *How might you use your reflections on this to build evidence for S38 and 39?*

We know that the original vision for the EYP role was that it would improve outcomes for all children (CWDC, 2010a). More recently, Tim Loughton, currently the Parliamentary Under Secretary for Children and Young Families, has reiterated the Government's commitment to 'improve the quality of the early years workforce and the development of a new generation of leaders for that sector' (Gaunt, 2010: 1). You have already played a crucial role in fulfilling this vision in your own personal journey towards EYPS and can look forward to ongoing professional support through your local EYP Network. Once you have achieved the status, part of your role will involve identifying colleagues who might be ready to begin their own pathways to EYPS. The overall rationale for a new understanding of 'professionalism' in the Early Years workforce is to improve workforce skills and develop a trained bank of graduate workers whose knowledge and competences will be key to effective delivery of EYFS provision. Your role in supporting and encouraging future leaders of practice is one you should embrace wholeheartedly.

C H A P T E R   S U M M A R Y

We have considered the gradual process towards a more professional understanding of Early Years practice and practitioners. We have identified some of the complexities in defining professionalism in the contemporary children's workforce but, nonetheless, highlighted components of professionalism in the Early Years as a distinctive knowledge base, set of values, training pathway and status in the community. In supporting the professional development of others, one of the most effective strategies is that of the EYP role-modelling an enthusiastic commitment to her/his own continuing development. The creation of a community of learners is a goal to which all EYPs should aspire as children, families, practitioners and the wider community engage in effective collaboration for the benefit of all. Within such a community, not only will children's learning and development needs be met effectively but so will those of the practitioners. In such an environment, future EYPs can be nurtured successfully and the role of the leader of practice will be embedded within the children's workforce. Such leaders will be able to demonstrate:

- reflective and reflexive practice in their own roles and skills in decision-making;

- sound knowledge and understanding of Early Years pedagogy: the holistic needs of all children from birth to five and competence in planning, implementing and monitoring within the framework of the Early Years Foundation Stage framework (DCFS, 2008a);

- strong values of the intrinsic worth of each child and all those in her/his world;

- the ability to role-model, lead and support others in high-quality practice;

- the ability to define a vision for practice within a setting;
- competence as an agent of change.

Self-assessment questions

1: Your own professional development journey

What do you understand now about the professional dimension to your role as EYP?

Issue for continuing professional development:	Why is it an issue for you now?	How might you address this need?

2: Leading and supporting others in their professional development

Question:	How do you know? Evidence from practice	Area for development
1. What is your experience of leading and supporting the professional development of colleagues in your setting?		
2. What opportunities do you create for reflective dialogue, as part of your role as leader of practice?		
3. In what ways are you helping the creation of a 'community of learners' in your setting?		
4. How do you encourage staff to engage in a process of regular self-evaluation/ appraisal of their practice?		
5. How do/might you identify potential future EYPs?		

FURTHER READING

Friedland, R. (2007) Professionalism in the Early Years. In Wild, M. and Mitchell, H. (eds) *Early Childhood Studies: Reflective Reader.* Exeter: Learning Matters.

Miller, L. and Cable, C. (2011) The changing face of professionalism in the Early Years. In Miller, L. and Cable, C. (eds) *Professionalization, Leadership and Management in the Early Years.* London: Sage (Chapter 1).

Appendix 1: Angela's professional journey

When I left school I completed my NNEB at college before holding positions in a range of settings: practitioner in private day nursery, nursery nurse in maintained nursery school (here I worked with an inspirational headteacher who had a profound impact on me in terms of children's creativity), supply work in Reception and Year 1 classes, pre-school leader of a 24-place setting.

When my daughter was born, I knew I wanted to stay at home with her but needed some income – so at this point became a registered childminder. I built up my reputation locally and really enjoyed building partnerships with a number of children and families. Reflecting on my early days of childminding I realise there were times, though, when I felt quite isolated.

Five years on, as a family, we relocated to a small rural farming village. I re-registered as a childminder but instantly found there did not seem to be the same need for a child-minding service within the village as there was a lot of extended family childcare provision. I minded two children on a very part-time basis but needed to find some other type of work for my own motivation and got a job-share position as leader of a local pre-school which I was able to combine with my childminding work.

Being a pre-school leader was a real challenge though very enjoyable. It was in carrying out the leadership role at pre-school that I became aware of the rapid changes within the Early Years sector. I considered carefully whether my NNEB qualification was going to be enough if I was going to stay long term in the sector and began to make tentative enquiries about furthering my qualifications.

I learned of the opportunity offered through the Sector Endorsed Early Years Foundation Degree (SEFDEY) which I commenced a few years ago. The following year, a couple of other families had made enquiries about my childminding services and I realised that I was keen just to focus on this role so I gave up the post of pre-school leader. I strongly believe young children are best cared for in a home-to-home environment.

I found the SEFDEY hard work, especially in juggling all the other demands in my life, but I loved it and feel I learnt loads and was constantly growing in confidence. Initially when faced with presentations and assignments I didn't know how I would get through but my tutors and workplace mentor helped me greatly and I found myself enjoying being in control and being able to express to others my passionate belief in the importance of the Early Years. I had become involved with my local childminding group and began to cascade information to them.

Just before I completed the SEFDEY, I applied for one of the Link Childminder positions in my area and was offered one of the posts. My earlier experience of isolation influences me very strongly in this role as I feel the early days of registration can be lonely and a daunting role for new childminders.

After I graduated from the SEFDEY with distinction, I wanted to explore appropriate ways of continuing to study and reflect on my practice. I learned of the opportunity to progress to a level 6 'top-up' programme at my local university. This was offered flexibly and the modules offered provided further opportunity for reflection on key aspects of Early Years practice and provision. I graduated with a BA Childhood Studies degree the following year.

A couple of years ago I heard that my local authority was recruiting tutors to deliver a new qualification for registered childminders. I was appointed and am thoroughly enjoying this role which I combine with my continued role as a childminder myself. The learners are very responsive and I adopt an interactive approach because as a part-time childminder myself, I am able to relate to real-life childminding situations. It has been a challenge working with three different stakeholders in the organisation of the course, but I have ensured that my presentation and delivery have been of a high quality.

I am now thinking 'what next?' I am hoping to prepare for EYPS validation and embark on further study to honours degree level. I would like to start the National Childminding Association Quality Assurance Scheme and continue my tutoring role perhaps developing this into a wider support role.

I certainly feel I have considerable knowledge and experience. However, throughout my long personal learning journey, I remain passionate about the field of childminding and home-based services. Whatever development my own career takes in the future, I genuinely love being with the children and want to continue this as part of my role.

Appendix 2: Pia is the leader of a pre-school playgroup and describes her 'learning community'

I qualified as a teacher in Sweden but when I moved to this country it was not possible to continue in this role without further (costly) training. At that point, I started working in a playgroup, as a waitress and as a railway conductor, while deciding what to do with my future. As it turned out I had my two children at that point and this led me, a little later, to join another playgroup, becoming treasurer and later joining the staff team.

As this proves, I hadn't until recently planned my professional development at all, but was instead driven by a wish to learn as much as I could about the field I'm working in and related issues – i.e. children's learning and development, parental involvement, etc. It was thus that I 'slid into' studying for a certificate in management. Part of this study entailed creating a professional development plan and it soon became apparent how useful this is; if nothing else, it highlights how much I actually do to keep up-to-date with current issues in my field.

I am currently working as a play leader in a small setting: a parent-managed pre-school playgroup, registered for 30 children. There is no traditionally carved career path, with opportunities for 'promotion' within the setting for me. I find that most of the professional development I undertake, and want to undertake, is to improve my practice in my current role. I am currently on the path of achieving EYPS and am not yet sure what other opportunities and challenges this might open up for me.

As the 'Learning for Life' and 'Every Child/Parent Matters' agendas further permeate the social structure, I sense that all Early Years settings are/will be working more and more with (or at least with the ideal of) parents as partners, which is the main reason I've worked within the pre-school movement. How then do I encourage others? When I reflect on this, I believe there are three key factors:

Vision: I encourage colleagues to commit to their own continuing professional development through my vision. I am aware that my formative years in Sweden have helped to shape my personal stance that everyone has equal rights to a fulfilling life, and one of the main reasons I've remained with the pre-school setting is that not only have I the privilege of learning with the children, I also do the same with their mums and dads and wider families. Being a 'new' parent is one of the greatest and at times hardest things and we see one of our important roles as building our setting's 'community' into a supportive network; we are stronger together. I believe that we are all learners (adults as well as children) and I want us to build 'a learning community'. This often leads to parents being encouraged to begin/continue studying as they continue or change career into a child-related one. Involvement on our committee may also lead to increased self-confidence and so to other study. Within our staff team, seven out of eleven of us started as parents in the setting, some with, but most without, any related qualifications. We now have six members of staff, myself included, who are studying – from level 1 right up to honours degree level and working towards EYPS.

Time: I believe that the committee's and my commitment to 'non-contact' time has a big part to play in the staff team development. We are paid to meet once a week, discussing not only the children's learning and planning for this, but also our own – short courses we have been on, reading materials, qualification studies, it all gets discussed. The support is there, not only from me, but from the whole team. This doesn't mean that we always agree – on the contrary – but then that is when you get a real chance to assess your own viewpoint and also to learn from each other. These meetings also offer time to discuss our learning ethos and the views of the children. We also have three in-house training sessions a year – looking at different issues, such as 'assessment and observation – the adult's role', 'planning', etc. Sometimes I decide on content, sometimes another staff member asks for a certain issue to be covered.

Leadership: I asked my staff individually about why they thought so many of us were studying at the moment and my role in this. Some mentioned that I acted as inspiration by studying myself. The reassurance that support was there helped, according to some, along with opportunities to share, discuss (and put into practice) things learnt. Some staff highlighted that how things were learnt was important. One member of staff said it helped to break down her resistance to further learning, when she realised that if others could do it, so could she. Nearly all staff also mentioned that the practical support I gave was important, advising on the different routes to qualifications. The most important factor that all the staff mentioned, however, was help with the financial side; me knowing the ins-and-outs of bursaries and other grants means that it's affordable for them – I have also negotiated with the committee, so that the setting now funds staff fully to achieve a Level 2 qualification, on the proviso that they stay with us for two years afterwards.

I have always seen as one aspect of my role the bringing into focus (for all adults – parents as well as staff) the great privilege of being allowed to, every day, share and be part of the miracle of the 'EUREKA-moments', the wide-eyed wonder and the awe of young learning – it's contagious and inspiring. I believe that taking time to discuss these moments every day not only celebrates each child's learning, but also encourages adults towards learning themselves – it's fun to learn!

References

Abbott, L. and Moylett, H. (1997) *Working with the Under-3s: Training and Professional Development.* Buckingham: Open University Press.

Allen, G. (2010) *Early Intervention: The Next Steps.* London: The Stationary Office.

Allen, S. and Whalley, M. E. (2010) *Supporting Pedagogy and Practice in Early Years Settings.* Exeter: Learning Matters.

Alliance for Inclusive Education (1990) Principles, available at http://www.allfie.org.uk/pages06/about/index.html (accessed 19 November 2007).

Anning, A. and Edwards, A. (2006) *Promoting Children's Learning from Birth to Five: Developing the New Early Years Professional.* Maidenhead: Open University Press.

Anning, A. and Edwards, A. (2010) Creating contexts for professional development. In Miller, L., Cable, C. and Goodliff, G. (eds) *Supporting Children's Learning in the Early Years* (2nd edn). London: Routledge.

Anning, A. and Hall, D. (2008) What was Sure Start and why did it matter? In Anning, A. and Ball, B. (eds) *Improving Services for Young Children: From Sure Start to Children's Centres.* London: Sage.

Anning, A., Cottrell, D., Frost, N., Green, J. and Robinson, M. (2006) *Developing Multiprofessional Teamwork for Integrated Children's Services.* Maidenhead: Open University Press.

Anning, A., Cullen, J. and Fleer, M. (2009) Research contexts across cultures. In Anning, A., Cullen, J. and Fleer, M. (eds) *Early Childhood Education: Society and Culture.* London: Sage.

Armstrong, M. (1994) *How to be an Even Better Manager.* London: Kogan Page.

Australia Early Childhood Association Inc. (1991) Australian Early Childhood Association Code of Ethics. *Australian Journal of Early Childhood,* 16 (1): 3–6.

Baldock, P., Fitzgerald, D. and Kay, J. (2009) *Understanding Early Years Policy* (2nd edn). London: Sage.

Ball, C. (1994) *Start Right: The Importance of Early Learning.* London: Royal Society for the Encouragement of the Arts, Manufacturing and Commerce.

Ball, M. and Anning, A. (2008) Building on good practice: lessons for Children's Centres. In Anning, A. and Ball, B. (eds) *Improving Services for Young Children: From Sure Start to Children's Centres.* London: Sage.

Bandura, A. (1977) *Social Learning Theory.* London: Prentice Hall.

Barnett, R. (2008) Critical professionalism in an age of supercomplexity. In Cunningham, B. (ed.) *Exploring Professionalism.* London: Bedford Way Papers.

Barron's Banking Dictionary (2010) *Change Agent [Internet].* Available from: http://www.answers.com/topic/change-agent (accessed 12 December 2010).

Bass, B. M. (1985) *Leadership and Performance Beyond Expectation.* New York: Free Press.

Bass, B. M. and Stodgill, R. M. (1990) *Handbook of Leadership: Theory, Research and Managerial Applications*. New York: Free Press.

Bax, M. (2001) Endeavours of Parents, Editorial in *Developmental Medicine and Child Neurology*, 43: 291.

Bee, H. and Boyd, D. (2006) *The Developing Child*. London: Pearson Education.

Belbin, M. (1993) *Team Roles at Work*. Cambridge: Belbin Associates.

Bennis, W. (1998) *On Becoming a Leader*. London: Arrow.

Bertram, T. and Pascal, C. (2002) *Early Years Education: An International Perspective*. London: QCA.

Bertram T., Pascal C., Bokhari, S., Gasper, M. and Holtermann, S. (2002) *Early Excellence Centre Pilot Programme Second Evaluation Report 2000–2001* (Research Report RR361). London: HMSO.

Blake, R. and Mouton, J. (1964) *The Managerial Grid: The Key to Leadership Excellence*. Houston: Gulf Publishing Co.

Bloom, P. J.(2000) How do we define director competence? *Childcare Information Exchange*, 138: 13–18.

Boddy, J., Cameron, C., Moss, P., Mooney, A., Petrie, P. and Statham, J. (2005) *Introducing Pedagogy into the Children's Workforce: Children's Workforce Strategy – A Response to the Consultation*. London: Thomas Coram Research Unit/Institute of Education, University of London.

Bolman, L. G. and Deal, T. E. (1997) *Reframing Organizations. Artistry, Choice and Leadership* (2nd edn). San Francisco: Jossey-Bass.

Bottery, M. (1990) *The Morality of the School*. London: Cassell.

Bottle, G. (2007) Research in the Early Years. In Nurse, A. (ed.) *The New Early Years Professional: Dilemmas and Debates*. London: David Fulton.

Bowman, B. T., Donovan, M. S. and Burns, M. S. (2000) *Eager to Learn: Educating our Pre-schoolers (Executive Summary)*. Washington, DC: National Academies Press. http://www.nap.edu/catalog/9745.html (accessed 30 December 2010).

British Educational Research Association Early Years Special Interest Group (2003) *Pedagogy, Curriculum, Adult Roles, Training and Professionalism*. London: BERA.

Broadhead, P., Wood, E. and Howard, J. (eds) (2010) *Play and Learning in the Early Years*. London: Sage.

Brock, A. (2006) Dimensions of early years professionalism – attitudes versus competences? Reflection Paper for Training Advancement and Cooperation in Teaching Young Children (TACTYC), available at http://www.tactyc.org.uk/pdfs/Reflection_brock.pdf (accessed: 30 November 2007).

Bronfenbrenner, U. (1979) *The Ecology of Human Development*. Cambridge, MA: Harvard University Press.

Brookfield, S. D. (1995) *Becoming a Critically Reflective Teacher*. San Francisco: Jossey-Bass.

Browne, E. (1995) *Handa's Surprise*. London: Walker Books.

Bruce, T., Whalley, M., Mairs, K., Arnold, C. and the Centre Team (1997) Case Study Two: a family centre. In Pascal, C. and Bertram, T. *Effective Early Learning: Case Studies in Improvement (Zero to Eight Series)*. London: Paul Chapman.

Bryman, A. (1986) *Charisma and Leadership in Organisations*. London: Routledge and Kegan Paul.

Burns, J. M. (1978) *Leadership*. New York: HarperCollins.

Burton, G. and Dimbleby, R. (1988) *Teaching Communication*. London: Routledge.

Bush, T. and Middlewood, D. (2005) *Leading and Managing People in Education*. London: Sage.

Cable, C. and Miller, L. (2011) A new professionalism. In Miller, L. and Cable, C. (eds) *Professionalization, Leadership and Management in the Early Years*. London: Sage.

Cable, C., Goodliff, G. and Miller, L. (2007) Developing reflective early years practitioners within a regulatory framework. *Malaysian Journal of Distance Education* 9 (2): 1–19.

Callan, S. (2006) What is mentoring? In Robbins, A. (ed.) *Mentoring in the Early Years*. London: Paul Chapman.

Carr, M. (2001) *Assessment in Early Childhood Settings: Learning Stories*. London: Sage/Paul Chapman.

Centre for the Development of Applied Research in Education (CeDARE) (2011) *First National Survey of Practitioners with Early Years Professional Status*. Leeds: Children's Workforce Development Council (CWDC).

Chakraborty, D. (2003) Leadership in the East and West: a few examples. *Journal of Human Values*, 9: 29–52.

Children's Workforce Development Council (CWDC) (2005) *Children's Workforce Strategy: A Consultation*. London: CWDC.

CWDC (2007) *Early Years Professional Status: Candidates' Handbook*. London: CWDC.

Children's Workforce Development Council (CWDC) (2010a) *On the Right Track – Guidance to the Standards for the Award of Early Years Professional Status*. Leeds: CWDC.

CWDC (2010b) Early Years Professional Status Pathways, available at http://www.cwdcouncil.org.uk/assets/0000/8608/EYPS_pathways.pdf (accessed 20 August 2010).

CWDC (2010c) Common Core of Skills and Knowledge for the Children's Workforce. Leeds: CWDC, available at http://www.cwdcouncil.org.uk/assets/0000/9007/CommonCore_FINAL.pdf (accessed 17 November 2010).

CWDC (2010d) All together, a better way of working – One Children's Workforce Framework poster. Leeds: CWDC.

Clark, K. E. and Clark, M. B. (eds) (1990). *Measures of Leadership*. Greensboro, NC: Center for Creative Leadership.

Claxton, G. and Carr, M. (2004) A framework for teaching learning: the dynamics of disposition. *Early Years*, 24 (1): 87–97.

Connolly, P. (2004) *Boys and Schooling in the Early Years*. London: RoutledgeFalmer.

Cooke, G. and Lawton, K. (2008) *For Love or Money: Pay, Progression and Professionalism in the Early Years Workforce.* London: Institute for Public Policy Research.

Costa, A. and Kallick, B. (1993) Through the lens of a critical friend. *Educational Leadership*, 51 (2), 49–51.

Covey, S. R. (1989) *The Seven Habits of Highly Effective People.* Boston, MA: Harvard Business School Press.

Cox, E. (1996) *Leading Women: Tactics for Making the Difference.* Sydney: Random House.

Craft, A. and Paige-Smith, A. (2008) Reflective practice. In Miller, L. and Cable, C. (eds) *Professionalism in the Early Years.* Oxon: Hodder Education.

Cuban, L. (1988) *The Managerial Imperative and the Practice of Leadership in Schools.* Albany, NY: State University of New York.

CUREE (2005) The National Framework for Mentoring and Coaching, available at http://www.curee-paccts.com/dynamic/curee75.jsp

Daly, M. Byers, E. and Taylor, W. (2004) *Early Years Management in Practice.* London: Heinemann.

Department for Children, Schools and Families (DCSF) (2007) Principles into Practice Cards. *The Early Years Foundation Stage.* Nottingham: DCSF.

DCSF (2008a) *Statutory Framework for the Early Years Foundation Stage.* Nottingham: DCSF.

DCSF (2008b) *Practice Guidance for the Early Years Foundation Stage.* Nottingham: DCSF.

DCSF (2008c) Effective Practice: Inclusive Practice. Resource on CD-Rom. *The Early Years Foundation Stage.* Nottingham: DCSF.

DCSF (2008d) Resource on CD-Rom. *The Early Years Foundation Stage.* Nottingham: DCSF.

DCSF (2008e) *Mark Making Matters: Young Children Making Meaning in All Areas of Learning and Development (National Strategies/Early Years).* Nottingham: DCSF.

DCSF (2009a) *Learning, Playing and Interacting – Good Practice in the Early Years Foundation Stage (National Strategies/Early Years).* Nottingham: DCSF.

DCSF (2009b) *Progress Matters: Reviewing and Enhancing Young Children's Development (National Strategies/Early Years).* Nottingham: DCSF.

DCSF (2010a) *Challenging Practice to Further Improve Learning, Playing and Interacting in the Early Years Foundation Stage (National Strategies/Early Years).* Nottingham: DCSF.

DCSF (2010b) *Finding and Exploring Young Children's Fascinations: Strengthening the Quality of Gifted and Talented Provision in the Early Years (National Strategies/Early Years).* Nottingham: DCSF.

DCSF (2010c) *Working Together to Safeguard Children: A Guide to Inter-agency Working to Safeguard and Promote the Welfare of Children.* Nottingham: DCSF.

Department for Education and Employment (DFEE) (2000) *Curriculum Guidance for the Foundation Stage.* London: Qualifications and Curriculum Authority (QCA).

Department of Education and Science (DES) (1990) *Starting with Quality: Report of the Committee of Inquiry into the Quality of Educational Experience Offered to Three and Four Year Olds* (Rumbold report). London: DES/HMSO.

Department for Education and Skills (DfES) (2001) *National Standards for Day Care and Childminding*. London: DfES.

Department for Education (DfE)/NatCen (2009–15) *Evaluation of Children's Centres in England (ECCE)*. Oxford: Department of Education, University of Oxford. Further information available at http://www.education.ox.ac.uk/research/fell/research/evaluation-of-children-centres-in-england-ecce/ (accessed 18 October 2010).

DfES (2002) *Birth to Three Matters: A Framework for Supporting Children in Their Earliest Years*. London: DfES.

DfES (2003) *Every Child Matters* (Green Paper). London: HMSO.

DfES (2004a) *Every Child Matters: Change for Children*. Nottingham: DfES.

DfES (2004b) *Statutory Guidance on Making Arrangements to Safeguard and Promote the Welfare of Children under section 11 of the Children Act 2004; Every Child Matters: Change for Children*. Nottingham: DfES.

DfES (2006) *Children's Workforce Strategy: The Government's Response to the Consultation*. Nottingham: DfES.

DfE (2010) *Government Moves to Free Up Children's Centre*, available at http://www.education. gov.uk/inthenews/inthenews/a0067775/government-moves-to-free-up-childrens-centres (accessed 30 November 2010).

DfES and Price Waterhouse Coopers (2007) *Independent Study of School Leadership*. Nottingham: DfES.

DfES/Sure Start (2007) *National Standards for Leaders of Sure Start Children's Centres*. Nottingham: DfES.

Dewey, J. (1933) *How We Think: A Restatement of the Relation of Reflective Thinking in the Educative Process*. Chicago: Henry Regnery.

Dewey, J. (1938) *Experience and Education*. New York: Simon and Schuster.

Dickerson, D. (2004) *Militant Mediator: Whitney M. Young Jnr.* Lexington, KY: The University Press of Kentucky.

Dickins, M. (2002) All About . . . Anti-Discriminatory Practice. *Nursery World*, 3: 15–22.

Doyle, M. E. and Smith, M. K. (1999) *Born and Bred? Leadership, heart and Informal Education*. London: YMCA George Williams College/The Rank Foundation.

Dryden, W. and Constantinou, D. (2004) *Assertiveness Step By Step*. London: Sheldon Press.

Dunlop, A.-W. (2002) *Scottish Nursery Teachers' Concepts of Leadership: Interim Report of Research in Progress*. Glasgow: University of Strathclyde.

Dunlop, A.-W. (2008) *A Literature Review on Leadership in the Early Years*, available at www.ltscotland. org.uk/Images/leadershipreview_tcm4–499140.doc (accessed 12 July 2010).

Eaton, S. (2006) Making Change Work. *Early Years Update*. October 2006. Available at http://www.teachingexpertise.com/articles/making-change-work-1401 (accessed 20 November 2010).

Ebbeck, M. and Waniganayake, M. (2003) *Early Childhood Professionals Leading Today and Tomorrow*. Sydney: Maclennan and Petty Ltd.

Edgington, M. (2004) *The Foundation Stage Teacher in Action* (3rd edn). London: Paul Chapman.

Edwards, C. P. and Forman, G.E. (eds.) (1993) *The Hundred Languages of Children: Reggio Emilia Approach to Early Childhood*. Norwood, New Jersey: Ablex Publishing Inc.

Fiedler, F. E. and Garcia, J. E. (1987) *New Approaches to Effective Leadership*. New York: John Wiley.

Fisher, A. (2001) *Critical Thinking: An Introduction*. Cambridge: Cambridge University Press.

Ford, S. (2009) Working in a multi-agency way. In Fabian, H. and Mould, C. (eds) *Development and Learning for Very Young Children*. London: Sage.

Friedland, R. (2007) Professionalism in the early years. In Wild, M. and Mitchell, H. (eds) *Early Childhood Studies: Reflective Reader*. Exeter: Learning Matters.

Garbarino, J. with Abramowitz, R. H. (1992) *Children and Families in the Social Environment*. Berlin: Aldine de Gruyter.

Gardner, H. (1983) *Frames of Mind: Theories of Multiple Intelligences*. New York: Basic Books.

Gardner, J. (1989) *On Leadership*. New York: Free Press.

Gaunt, C. (2010) Strategy ahead for workforce leaders. *Nursery World Online*, 21 December 2010. Available at http://www.nurseryworld.co.uk/news/bulletin/NurseryWorldUpdate/article/1047453/?DCMP=EMC-CONNurseryWorldUpdate (accessed 21 December 2010).

Ghaye, A. and Ghaye, K. (1998) *Teaching and Learning through Critical Reflective Practice*. London: David Fulton.

Gillen, T. (1995) *Positive Influencing Skills*. London: Chartered Institute of Personnel Development.

Glazzard, J., Chadwick, D., Webster, A. and Percival, J. (2010) *Assessment for Learning in the Early Years Foundation Stage*. London: Sage.

Goleman, D. (1996) *Emotional Intelligence: Why It Can Matter More than IQ*. London: Bloomsbury.

Greenfield, S. (2011) Working in multidisciplinary teams. In Miller, L. and Cable, C. (eds) *Professionalization, Leadership and Management in the Early Years*. London: Sage.

Hawkey, K. (2006) Emotional intelligence and mentoring in pre-service teacher education: a literature review. *Mentoring and Tutoring*, 14 (2): 137–47.

Hall, V. (1996) *Dancing on the Ceiling*. London: Paul Chapman.

Hallet, E. (2004) The reflective practitioner. In Macleod-Brudenell, I. (ed.) *Advanced Care and Education Level 4 and 5*. Oxford: Heinemann Educational.

Harris, A., Day, C. and Hadfield, M. (2003) Teachers' perspectives on effective school leadership. *Teachers and Teaching: Theory and Practice*, 9 (1): 67–77.

Heifetz, R. A. (1994) *Leadership Without Easy Answers*. Cambridge, MA: Belknap Press.

Hersey, P. and Blanchard, K. H. (1988) *Management and Organisational Behaviour* (2nd edn). Englewood Cliffs, NJ: Prentice-Hall.

Hirsch, D. (2007) *Chicken and Egg: Child Poverty and Educational Inequalities*. Child Poverty Action Group Briefing Paper, London: CPAG.

Home Office (2003) *The Victoria Climbié Inquiry: Report of an Inquiry by Lord Laming*. Norwich: Her Majesty's Stationery Office.

Horne, M. and Stedman Jones, D. (2001) *Leadership: The Challenge for All?* London: Institute of Management.

Howard, J. (2010) The developmental and therapeutic potential of play: re-establishing teachers as play professionals. In Moyles, J. (ed.) *The Excellence of Play* (3rd edn). Maidenhead: Open University Press.

Hughes, E. (2005) *Collected Poems for Children.* London: Faber and Faber.

Hujala, E. (2004) Dimensions of leadership in the childcare context. *Scandinavian Journal of Educational Research*, 48 (1): 53–71.

Isaksen, S. and Tidd, J. (2006) *Meeting the Innovation Challenge*. Chichester: John Wiley and Sons.

Karpf, A. (2007) Forget phonics – that's for teachers. Parents have fun with your kids. *The Guardian Family Supplement* (3 November), available at http://lifeandhealth.guardian.co.uk/family/story/0,,2216141,00.html (accessed 15 April 2008).

Laming, H. (2003) *The Victoria Climbié Enquiry: Report of an Enquiry by Lord Laming*. London: HMSO.

Lancaster, P. (2010) Listening to young children: enabling children to be seen and heard. In Pugh, G. and Duffy, B. (eds) *Contemporary Issues in the Early Years*. London: Sage.

Lave, J. and Wenger, E. (1991) *Situated Learning: Legitimate Peripheral Participation*. Cambridge: Cambridge University Press.

Law, S. and Glover, D. (2000) *Educational Leadership and Learning: Practice, Policy and Research*. Buckingham: Open University Press.

Lee, M. (2010) Professional development in the early years: the impact of Early Years Professional Status. From *Early Years Update*, Teaching Expertise, October 2010, available at http://www.teachingexpertise.com/articles/professional-development-early-years-impact-early-years-professional-status-10117 (accessed 12 January 2011).

Leeson, C. (2007) In praise of reflective practice. In Willan, J., Parker-Rees, R. and Savage, J. *Early Childhood Studies* (2nd edn). Exeter: Learning Matters.

Lindon, J. (2006) *Equality in Early Childhood: Linking Theory and Practice*. London: Hodder Arnold.

Lloyd, E. and Hallet, E. (2010) Professionalising the early childhood workforce in England: work in progress or missed opportunity? *Contemporary Issues in Early Childhood*, 11 (1): 75–88.

Louis, K. S. S., Marks, H. and Kruse, S. (1996) Teachers' professional communities in restructuring schools. *American Educational Research Journal*, 33 (4): 757–98.

Luckock, B. (2010) A 'whole system' for the whole child? Integrated services, interprofessional working and the development of effective practice with children and families. In Robb, M. and Thomson, R. (eds) *Critical Practice with Children and Young People*. Milton Keynes: The Open University.

Mann, R. D. (1959) A review of the relationship between personality and performance in small groups. *Psychological Bulletin*, 66 (4): 241–70.

Maslow, A. (1968) *Towards a Psychology of Being* (2nd edn). New York: D. Van Nostrand Co.

van Maurik, J. (2001) *Writers on Leadership*. London: Penguin.

McCauley, C. D., Moxley, R. and van Velsor, E. (eds) (1998) *The Centre for Creative Leadership Handbook of Leadership Development*. San Francisco: Jossey-Bass.

McGregor, D. (1970) *The Human Side of Enterprise*. New York: McGraw-Hill.

Mehrabian, A. (1981) *Silent Messages: Implicit Communication of Emotions and Attitudes.* Belmont, CA: Wadsworth.

Miller, L. (2008) Developing professionalism within a regulatory framework in England: challenges and possibilities. *European Early Childhood Education Research Journal*, 16 (2): 255–68.

Miller, L. and Pound, L. (2011) Taking a critical perspective. In Miller, L. and Pound, L. (eds) *Theories and Approaches to Learning in the Early Years*. London: Sage.

Moyles, J. (2001) Passion, paradox and professionalism in Early Years education. *Early Years*, 21 (2): 81–95.

Moyles, J. (ed.) (2005) *The Excellence of Play* (2nd edn). Maidenhead: Open University Press.

Moyles, J. (2006) *Effective Leadership and Management in the Early Years*. Maidenhead: Open University Press.

Moyles, J. (ed.) (2010) *The Excellence of Play* (3rd edn). Maidenhead: Open University Press.

Moyles, J., Adams, S. and Musgrove, A. (2002) *SPEEL: The Study of Pedagogical Effectiveness in Early Learning*. Research Report 363, London: DfES.

Muijs, D., Aubrey, C., Harris, A. and Briggs, M. (2004) How do they manage? A review of the research in early childhood. *Journal of Early Childhood Research*, 2: 157, available at http://ecr.sage pub.com/cgi/content/abstreact/2/2/157 (accessed 19 October 2007).

Munro, J. (2011) *The Munro Report of Child Protection Interim Report: The Child's Journey*, available at http://www.education.gov.uk/munroreview/ (accessed 3 February 2011).

National Children's Bureau (2010) *NCB launches new 'Firm Foundations' early years campaign*, available at http://www.ncb.org.uk/campaigning/media_news/2010/jan_to_jun/firm_foundations_campaign.aspx (accessed 18 October 2010).

National College and Children's Workforce Network (2009) *Building Effective Integrated Leadership*. Nottingham: National College.

Neugabauer, B. and Neugabauer, R. (eds) (1998) *The Art of Leadership: Managing Early Childhood Organisations* (vol. 2). Perth, Australia: Childcare Information Exchange.

New Zealand Ministry of Education (1996) *Te Whāriki: Early Childhood Curriculum*. Wellington, NZ: Ministry of Education.

Noone, M. (1996) *Mediation*. London: Cavendish.

Nurse, A. (ed.) (2007) *The New Early Years Professional: Dilemmas and Debates*. London: David Fulton.

Nutbrown, C. (1996) *Respectful Educators – Capable Learners: Children's Rights and Early Education*. London: Paul Chapman.

Oberhuemer, P. (2008) Who is an early years professional? Reflections on policy diversity in Europe. In Miller, L. and Cable, C. (eds) *Professionalism in the Early Years*. London: Hodder and Stoughton.

Oberhuemer, P. and Scheryer, I. (2008) What professional? *Children in Europe: Aiming High. A Professional Workforce for Early Years*, 15: 9–12.

Office for Standards in Education (Ofsted) (2008) Leading to Excellence, available at http://www.ofsted.gov.uk/Ofsted-home/Leading-to-excellence (accessed 21 December 2010).

Paul, R. and Elder, L. (2006) *Critical Thinking Tools for Taking Charge of Your Learning.* Upper Saddle River, NJ: Prentice Hall.

Payler, J. (2005) Opening and closing interactive spaces: early years pedagogy and four year old children's contributions to it in two English settings. Conference Paper for British Educational Research Association Annual Conference, University of Glamorgan, 14–17 September 2005.

Peeters, J. and Vandenbroeck, M. (2011) Childcare practitioners and the process of professionalization. In Miller, L. and Cable, C. (eds) *Professionalization, Leadership and Management in the Early Years*. London: Sage.

Pen Green Team (2007) All about . . . Working with Parents. Available on EYFS CD-ROM: The Early Years Foundation Stage, file://D:/resources/downloads/2.2_a.pdf

Pinnington, A. (2009) *Pirate Pete's Potty Book.* London: Ladybird Books.

Pound, L. (2005) Management, leadership and teamwork. In Dryden, L., Forbes, R., Mukherji, P., Pound, L., Chawla-Duggan, R., Joshi, U., Menon, C. and Trodd, L. *Essential Early Years*. London: Hodder Arnold.

Pound, L. (2008) Leadership in the early years. In Miller, L. and Cable, C. *Professionalism in the Early Years.* Oxon: Hodder Education.

Powell, J. (2007) Multi-agency development and issues of communication. In Nurse, A. (ed.) *The New Early Years Professional: Dilemmas and Debates* London: David Fulton.

Ramey, S. L., Ramey, C. T., Philips, M. M., Lanzi, R. G., Brezausek, C., Katholi, C. R., Snyders, S. and Lawrence, F. L. (2000) *Head Start Children's Entry into Public School: A Report on the National Head Start/Public School Early Childhood Transition Study*. Birmingham, AL: Curtan International Research Centre.

Ranson , R., Halpin, D., Nixon, J. and Seddon, T. (2004) Editorial. *London Review of Education*, 2 (3): 163–69. In Petrie, P. (2005) Extending pedagogy. *Journal of Education for Teaching*, 31 (4): 293–96.

Robinson, M. (2008) *Child Development from Birth to Eight: A Journey through the Early Years*. Maidenhead: Open University Press.

Rodd, J. (1997) Learning to be leaders: perceptions of early childhood professionals about leadership roles and responsibilities. *Early Years*, 18 (1): 40–46.

Rodd, J. (1998) *Leadership in Early Childhood: The Pathway to Professionalism* (2nd edn). Sydney: Allen and Unwin.

Rodd, J. (2006) *Leadership in Early Childhood* (3rd edn). Maidenhead: Open University Press.

Rogoff, B. (1991) Social interaction as apprenticeship in thinking: guided participation in spatial planning. In Resnick, L., Levine, J. and Teasley, S. (eds) *Perspectives on Socially Shared Cognition*. Washington DC: APA.

Rosener, J. B. (1997). Sexual static. In Grint, K. (ed.) *Leadership: Classical, Contemporary and Critical Approaches*. Oxford: Oxford University Press.

Sadler, P. (1997) *Leadership*. London: Kogan Page.

Samuelsson, I. and Carlsson, M. (2008) The playing learning child: towards a pedagogy of early childhood. *Scandinavian Journal of Educational Research*, 52 (6): 623–41.

Schön, D. (1983) *The Reflective Practitioner*. New York: Basic Books.

Schrag, L., Nelson, E. and Siminowsky, T. (1985) Helping employees cope with change. *Child Care Information Exchange* (September): 3–6.

Senge, P. M. (1994) *The Fifth Discipline*. Cambridge, MA: MIT Press.

Shaw, M. E. (1976) *Group Dynamics: The Psychology of Small Groups* (2nd edn). New York: McGraw-Hill.

Shea, M. (1993) *Personal Impact, Presence, Para-Language and the Art of Good Communication*. London: Sinclair-Stevenson.

Simpson, D. (2010) Being professional: conceptualising early years professionals in England. *European Early Childhood Education Research Journal*, 18 (1): 5–14.

Siraj-Blatchford, I. (2010) The EPPE settings in the context of English pre-schoools. In Sylva, K., Melhuish, E., Sammons, P., Siraj-Blatchford, I. and Taggart, B. (eds) *Early Childhood Matters: Evidence from the Effective Pre-school and Primary Education project*. London: Sage.

Siraj-Blatchford, I. and Clark, P. (2000) *Supporting Identity, Diversity and Language in the Early Years*. Buckingham: Open University Press.

Siraj-Blatchford, I. and Manni, L. (2007) *Effective Leadership in the Early Years Sector: The ELEYS Study*. London: Institute of Education, University of London.

Siraj-Blatchford, I., Sylva, K., Muttock, S., Gilden, R. and Bell, D. (2002) *Researching Effective Pedagogy in the Early Years (REPEY)*. DfES Research Report 356, London: DfES/HMSO.

Smith, A. and Langston, A. (1999) *Managing Staff in Early Years Settings*. London: Routledge.

Solley, K. (2003) What do early childhood leaders do to maintain and enhance the significance of the early years? Paper presented at the Institute of Education, University of London, 22 May, available at www.early-education.org.uk/resources/wdeyl95.doc (accessed 16 November 2007).

Spillane, J., Halverson, R. and Diamond, J. (2004) Towards a theory of leadership practice: a distributed perspective. *Journal of Curriculum Studies*, 36 (1): 3–34.

Stacey, M. (2009) *Teamwork and Collaboration in Early Years Settings*. Exeter: Learning Matters.

Stephen, C. (2010) Pedagogy: the silent partner in early years learning. *Early Years*, 30 (1): 15–28.

Stevenson, D. (2008) What is a 'change agent'? available at http://it.toolbox.com/blogs/original-thinking/what-is-a-change-agent-23764 (accessed 12 December 2010).

Stogdill, R. M. (1948) Personal factors associated with leadership. a survey of the literature. *Journal of Psychology*, 25: 35–71.

Straker, D. (2010) *Planning for Change* available at http://changingminds.org/disciplines/change_management/planning_change/planningchange.htm (accessed 2 January 2011).

Sure Start Keighley (2005) *Evaluation Report Summary* (one of three evaluations commissioned by Sure Start Keighley and carried out by Leeds University). Keighley: Sure Start Keighley.

Sutherland, M. (2005) *Gifted and Talented in the Early Years*. London: Sage/Paul Chapman.

Sylva, K. (2010a) Quality in early childhood settings. In Sylva, K., Melhuish, E., Sammons, P., Siraj-Blatchford, I. and Taggart, B. (eds) *Early Childhood Matters: Evidence from the Effective Pre-school and Primary Education project*. London: Sage.

Sylva, K. (2010b) Rethinking the evidence base for early years policy and practice. In Sylva, K., Melhuish, E., Sammons, P., Siraj-Blatchford, I. and Taggart, B. (eds) *Early Childhood Matters: Evidence from the Effective Pre-school and Primary Education project*. London: Sage.

Sylva, K., Melhuish, E. C., Sammons, P., Siraj-Blatchford, I. and Taggart, B. (2004) *The Effective Provision of Pre-School Education (EPPE) Project: Final Report*. London: DfEE/Institute of Education, University of London.

Sylva, K., Siraj-Blatchford, I., Melhuish, E. C., Lewis, K., Morahan, M. and Sadler, S. (1999) *The Effective Provision of Pre-School Education (EPPE) Project: Technical Paper 6A – Characteristics of pre-school environments*. London: DfEE/Institute of Education, University of London.

Sylva, K., Siraj-Blatchford, I., Taggart, B., Sammons, P., Melhuish, E., Elliot, K. and Totsika, V. (2006) Capturing quality in early childhood through environmental rating scales. *Early Childhood Research Quarterly*, 21: 76–92.

Teather, H. (2011) Upskilling the workforce: the minister's view. *Nursery World*, 27: 12.

Tickell, C. (2011) *The Early Years: Foundations for Life, Health and Learning*. London: DfE. Available at www.education.gov.uk/tickellreview (accessed 31 March 2011).

Thornton, K. R. (2005) *Courage, Commitment and Collaboration: Notions of Leadership in the New Zealand ECE 'Centres of Innovation'*. Victoria: University of Wellington (unpublished M.Ed. thesis).

Thornton, L. and Brunton, P. (2007) *Bringing the Reggio Approach to your Early Years Practice*. London: David Fulton.

Tovey, H. (2007) *Playing Outdoors: Spaces and Places Risk and Challenge*. Maidenhead: Open University Press.

Trodd, L. (2005) Launching into learning: becoming a reflective practitioner. In Dryden, L., Forbes, R., Mukherji, P., Pound, L., Joshi, U., Chawla-Duggan, R., Menon, C. and Trodd, L. *Essential Early Years*. London: Hodder Arnold.

Tuckman, B. W. (1965) Developmental sequence in small groups. *Psychological Bulletin*, 63: 384–99.

Tuckman, B. W. and Jensen, M. A. (1977) Stages of small group development revisited. *Group and Organisational Studies*, 2: 419–27.

United Nations (1989) *Convention on the Rights of the Child*, available at www2.ohchr.org/English/law/crc.htm (accessed 4 January 2011).

Walden, D. and Shiba, S. (2001) *Four Practical Revolutions in Management Systems for Creating Organisational Capabilities* (2nd edn). New York: Productivity Press.

Waniganayake, M. (2006) Preface. to Rodd, J. *Leadership in Early Childhood*. Maidenhead: Open University Press.

Wenger, E. (1998) *Communities of Practice*. Cambridge: Cambridge University Press.

Whalley, M. (2002) Creative waves: National College of School Leadership discussion paper on future schools. Keynote address at British Educational Research Association Annual Conference, 2002, available at http://www.ncsl.org.uk/media/F7B/95/randd-futures-creative-waves.pdf (acessed 31 October 2007).

Whalley, M. (2005a) Developing leadership approaches for early years settings. Pen Green: unpublished lecture, available at www.ncsl.org.uk/media/F58/76/communityleadership-together-m-whalley.ppt (accessed 30 November 2007).

Whalley, M. (2005b) Leadership professional development for integrated services. Unpublished keynote address for Daycare Trust Annual Conference, 2005, available at www.daycaretrust.org.uk/mod/fileman/files/Margy_Whalley_web_version.ppt (accessed 7 December 2007).

Whalley, M. and the Pen Green Centre Team (2007) *Involving Parents in Their Children's Learning* (2nd edn). London: Paul Chapman.

Whalley, M., Whitaker, P., Wyles, G. and Harris, P. (2005) *An Enquiry into the Impact of a Leadership Development Programme on Leaders of Integrated Early Years Centres*. Corby: Pen Green.

Whalley, M. E. (2011) Leading and Managing in the Early Years. In Miller, L. and Cable, C. (eds) *Professionalization, Leadership and Management in the Early Years*. London: Sage.

Whitaker, P. (2004) *NPQICL Pedagogical Leadership*. Nottingham: NCSL.

Willan, J. (2007) Research projects in early childhood studies: students' active explorations of children's worlds. In Willan, J., Parker-Rees, R. and Savage, J. *Early Childhood Studies* (2nd edn). Exeter: Learning Matters.

Wright, P. (1996) *Managerial Leadership*. London: Routledge.

Yukl, G. and Chavez, C. (2002) Influence tactics and leader effectiveness. In Neider, L. L. and Schriesheim, C. (eds) *Leadership*. Greenwich, CT: Information Age Publishing.

Index